Garden Colour

Sue Fisher

Garden Colour

hamlyn

First published in Great Britain in 2003 by Hamlyn, a
division of Octopus Publishing Group Ltd, 2–4 Heron
Quays, London E14 4JP

© Octopus Publishing Group Ltd 2003

Distributed in the United States and Canada by
Sterling Publishing Co., Inc.
387 Park Avenue South, New York, NY 10016-8810

Sue Fisher has asserted her moral right to be
identified as the author of this work.

ISBN 0 600 60418 7

A CIP catalogue record for this book is available from
the British Library

Printed and bound in China

10 9 8 7 6 5 4 3 2 1

contents

introduction

Colour **stimulates** and soothes, excites and **relaxes**. It orchestrates our moods in subtle but far-reaching ways. Without **colour** our lives would be very much more dull and we would see our gardens solely for their utility and not their beauty. Beyond the practicalities of 'somewhere to sit, somewhere to play, somewhere to grow things', we look to our gardens as somewhere we can express ourselves – where, whether we consider ourselves **artistic** or not, we can paint a beautiful **picture** with nature's colours. Used thoughtfully, colour brings **harmony** to quiet corners, adds **drama** and interest and can even be used to create **illusions**. Perhaps most importantly, it allows us to stamp our own personalities on the garden.

Now, there is more potential for colouring our gardens than ever before. We can choose from an unparalleled range of planting styles and colour schemes, and with tens of thousands of plants at our disposal, we are encouraged to become ever more adventurous, experimenting with new varieties of old favourites and exciting exotics.

But freedom of choice comes hand in hand with confusion – at the sheer variety of colour and what to plant where and with what. The often-quoted phrase that there are no clashes in nature may once have been true, but no longer – hybridizers have created all manner of spectacular shades that clash violently together, sometimes even on the same plant! Yet there is no need to be overwhelmed. By tackling the subject in a logical way, this book takes you through the whole process from start to finish, enabling you to create all sorts of beautiful plantings in a way that is simple and worry-free.

where do I start?

Colour is a very personal matter. There are no 'right' and 'wrong' approaches to colour – just fashions – and picking *your* favourite colours is the first and most important step to take.

As you are looking for inspiration for the garden you have probably already had a little practice in choosing colours for your house or apartment. Looking at the colours you choose to surround yourself with in your home is a good starting point for doing the same for your garden. If your house is decorated in bold, brilliant colours, you're unlikely to favour soft pastels in the garden, and vice versa.

However, there are important differences as well as similarities between using colour inside and outside the house. In a garden the emphasis is less on individual colours, but rather on how they are put together. Partly because of the predominance of green as a 'buffer', you can use all sorts of colour mixes that you might not consider indoors. But an unconsidered jumble creates a confusion of looks and moods, and detracts from the overall appearance of a garden. So, does the adage 'Less is more' apply? Sometimes, but a whole garden that is made up of plants using only a single colour can start to look monotonous and flat. The route to success in the garden is to combine several colours that work well together.

An indoor colour scheme can usually be created – or rectified – by a weekend spent with paint pots and brushes, but seeing the results of 'painting' in the garden takes much longer. Some plants, it is true, will come into their own in a few months, but most will develop over the years, growing in stature and beauty with the passage of time.

right: Less is more: restricting a scheme to just a few colours gives great impact.

solutions from indoors

By looking at the interior of your home, and even your clothes, you can find clues to what you'll enjoy in the garden – a great source of inspiration that can fast-track you in the right direction.

hallway/entrance room First impressions count. Your front garden, even if it is just a couple of pots flanking the front door, is a telling introduction to you and your home. What do you want to say?

kitchen Do you like bright colour or soft shades as a wake-up call? Relate these shades to the view outside from your breakfast spot or for key garden viewpoints at other times of day.

living room Most time is spent here so these colours can be used as inspiration for the most-used parts of the garden.

bedroom The ultimate place for relaxation. Relate these colours to places outside where you'll sit and relax.

you are what you wear Open your wardrobe doors and analyse what lies within: pastels, vibrant shades, or businesslike monochrome?

take a look at colour

Sit back and think about colour in its broadest sense. As a general guide, colours fall into two main groups – strong, warm shades and soft, cool ones. Strong ones like red, orange, bright yellow and purple are most dynamic, stepping up the tempo to create a sense of drama, excitement and exhilaration. By comparison, soft blues, mauves, pale yellows and pinks are calm and peaceful, and blend gently into the landscape. The impression you create in a space will depend on choice of hues and shades and the way you put them together, and this can alter from season to season.

With all this in mind, have a look at the pictures throughout the book and make a note of which colours catch your eye and which make your toes curl. Most people have a preference for strong or soft colours, but if you're not sure then go for the easy approach

of omission rather than inclusion: strike off the absolute no-goes and work with what is left.

Once you have a sense of which colours you prefer, you can consider how these might work in combination. It's a matter of personal taste whether you find a scheme subtle or boring, but to achieve the best effects in your garden you need to exploit the way colours naturally work together. Chapter 1 (Exploring Colour Combinations) shows how shades and tones within a single colour have their own moods and qualities, and how harmonies and contrasts create different impressions. Chapters 2 (Your Garden Palette) and 3 (Colourful Foliage) are full of ideas for specific combinations of both flowers and foliage in different seasons, and the case studies on pages 122–29 demonstrate how these can be pulled together into a variety of finished

schemes. Finally, turn to Chapter 7 (Planting) to see how to build up your own successful plantings of your own.

put the garden in charge

The conditions in your garden are very likely to narrow down your choice of colours, which does actually make the job easier. Bear in mind that site and soil should *always* be the prime factors that influence your choice of plants, for there is no point in making life difficult by trying to grow plants that dislike their environment. The plants chosen for this book are all good garden performers, and you can be assured that the selection does not include any of those tempestuous prima donnas that need the horticultural equivalent of intensive care to survive. Then there are other

factors, such as size and aspect, to be taken into account, as well as the effect of light at different times of day and year, all of which are considered in Chapter 4 (Infinite Variety). This is also the chapter to inspire you to play with colour to gain the illusion of extra space, to blur boundaries and to bring a touch of theatricality to your plot.

other colour cues

Apart from plants, colour in the garden comes from many other sources, from walls and fences to garden furniture and ornamental features. Chapter 6 investigates outdoor decorating, illustrating how the extensive selection of coloured wood stains and an increasingly imaginative range of 'flooring' can transform paths, terraces and garden

buildings. It also takes a creative look at unchangeable features, such as neighbouring walls and large trees, and has a host of ideas for colourful mulches and colour-coordinated container planting.

If at all unsure about which colours to choose, take your cue from nature. Chapter 5 (Colour Through the Year) is a guide through the colours that naturally predominate at different times of the year. Work in tune with the seasons and you won't go wrong. Use this chapter as a checklist to be sure of having a garden to enjoy every month of the year. The easiest mistake is to buy lots of plants that look good in spring and summer – the time when shopping for plants is most fun – and to end up with very little that looks good at other times. The more melancholy seasons are just when we need a little colour in our lives.

far left: Compared to more muted shades, bright colours instantly leap out and catch the eye.

left: Flowers in different shades of the same colour are wonderfully harmonious.

above: Completely contrasting colours look best with plenty of green as a buffer.

exploring colour combinations

all the colours of the rainbow

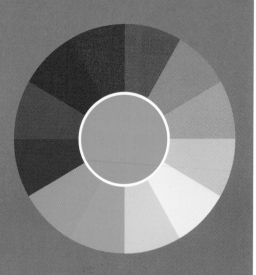

To get the most out of colour, it's useful to know a little about why colours work well in certain combinations but not in others. The colours of a rainbow always appear in the same distinct order, which is known as the spectrum. When this graded line of colours is bent round into a circle, it is known as the colour wheel. On one half are the 'warm' colours – red, orange, yellow and lime-green – and the other are the 'cool' colours – green, blue and purple. Colours that are adjacent to each other have a greatest similarity and together form a harmony, while pairs on opposite sides of the wheel have the least in common and form contrasts. Harmonies are always easy on the eye, while contrasts are bold and striking – both can be used to great effect in the garden.

strong or soft?

The world of colour is made up of an infinite number of shades, tones and hues, and the strength or depth of a colour makes a great deal of difference to how we regard it. A colour's strength needs to be taken into account regardless of whether you want to create harmonies or contrasts. Strong, deep colours are very intense, while paler ones look as though they have been diluted with white or grey. Harmonies work best made up of either soft shades or deep colours rather than a mixture of the two.

Marry a strong yellow with an equally bright orange, for example, and you get a bold combination that works; substitute a pale apricot and the effect is unbalanced, making the yellow appear brassy and the subtle shade of orange insipid.

The same can apply to contrasts, but not always: rich blue looks really stunning with a bold, bright yellow, where a pale blue only looks okay – but the pale apricot that previously looked washed-out against the strong yellow now makes an appealing contrast with the rich blue.

buffer colours

While the colour harmonies or contrasts are the chief players in a planting scheme, too much undiluted colour loses its appeal. Just as a meal of rich food needs the accompaniment of bread or vegetables to be savoured to the full, so a planting scheme needs to be woven through with neutral 'buffer' colours such as white, cream or silver-grey. In the garden, green is also a buffer colour.

breaking the rules – why it works

While colours are guaranteed to work with each other in certain harmonies or contrasts, there is no need to stick to these ones if you fancy being adventurous and creating a really startling colour clash or shock. Try really bright colours – vivid magenta with scarlet; glowing orange with hot pink; purple with orange; deep pink and bright yellow. For these dramatic colour combinations to look effective, make a small group of plants solely of these colours so the effect is an obviously created one, or it will look to have been made accidentally.

how to choose colour combinations you like

Exploring your favourite colour combinations – and eliminating those you don't like – is a project to take plenty of time over. This is a great way of getting a feel for the way in which colours can work together without spending any money on buying plants.

1 Begin by collecting together a good selection of well-illustrated plant catalogues – old ones from gardening friends will do, or order some from the advertisements you'll find in gardening magazines. You'll also need a decent-sized pinboard or a large piece of thick cardboard, along with lots of drawing pins.

2 Cut out good pictures showing close-ups of flowers or leaves until you have at least a dozen of each of the flower and foliage colours covered on pages 22–73. Sort them into piles according to their colours.

3 With the board lying flat, make up groups of different colour harmonies and contrasts – look through this book for a few ideas. Try putting a colour into several different groups and see how the effect changes according to the combination.

4 When you have settled on some combinations that you like, pin the pictures into place. Then stand the board somewhere prominent for several days so you can consider the results and juggle the pictures further. Also, take it outside in different spots around the garden and see the effect that sun or shade has on colour and your personal perception of it.

above: Using muted shades of opposing colours makes for a more subtle contrast.

in search of inspiration

● To get a feel for the sorts of colours that you like, there's absolutely no substitute for seeing plants in the flesh. Visiting some of the many gardens open to the public is a brilliant way of doing this and makes for a great day out too.

● Buy or borrow a good guide to the larger gardens open to the public – these larger gardens tend to have plants that are clearly labelled, so you can make a note of your favourites. You'll also need a camera, notebook and pen.

● Many of these gardens are landscaped on a grand scale and it's all too easy to become distracted by the big picture. But focus on the smaller picture instead and look at the colouring of groups of plants – anything from a simple partnership to a planting of a dozen or so different varieties. Take photographs of the combinations you like and note down the plant names, so you can re-create a similar grouping at home.

left: Opposites on the colour wheel create a sharp and distinct contrast.

harmonies

colour harmonies ...

... are closely related to each other
... are safe and easy to create
... can be either soft and calm or strong and bold

To build up a harmonious planting combination, begin by choosing a **key colour** on which to base the scheme. Decide on whether you want a **hot, vibrant** colour such as red, orange or yellow, or a **cool, calming** one like blue or green. Then, choose from the **adjacent colours** on the colour wheel. Weave through **greens** and **neutrals** to make up a beautifully **balanced** scheme. The following examples are based around the three principal or primary colours, though there can be endless variations on colour **harmonies**.

right: Note how the red sedums 'leap' forward in this otherwise harmonious mix of mauve flowers and buff grasses.

harmonies with blue

Subtle and restful, blue works well in many combinations and there is a plentiful range of plants to choose from. As buffer colours, choose silver-green and blue-green foliage plants which pick out the tones in the flowers, as well as plenty of plain green leaves.

● Blue, mauve and purple make a delightful mix of cool summer colour. Try the drumstick heads of the decorative onion *Allium* 'Purple Sensation' with *Lavandula angustifolia* 'Munstead' and the perennial wallflower *Erysimum* 'Bowles Mauve'.

● Shades of blue along with silver and grey foliage create a very soft and laid-back planting. Try a blue-green hosta such as 'Halcyon' with the ornamental grass *Elymus arenarius* and blue primulas or the deep azure *Veronica peduncularis* 'Georgia Blue'.

● Pink and blue in soft shades is a classic combination. Try catmint (*Nepeta* x *faassenii*) with *Lavatera* x *clementii* 'Blushing Bride'

● Strong pinks and blues look much warmer and eye-catching. Try *Anchusa* 'Loddon Royalist' with a deep pink rose such as 'Gertrude Jekyll'.

above: Citrus shades of orange and yellow sing with life and sunshine.

harmonies with yellow

The sunny associations of yellow make it a popular choice for colour schemes. As a buffer, weave through plenty of light to mid-green foliage but avoid dark evergreens that would give a rather sombre touch.

● Pale yellow makes a glowing harmony with soft peach and apricot. Try *Anthemis tinctoria* 'E.C. Buxton' with one of the many peach-coloured roses, such as 'Sweet Dream'.

● Bright yellow with orange and lime-green combine in a lively and upbeat harmony. Try yellow argyranthemums (marguerites) with the lime-tasselled *Amaranthus caudatus* 'Viridis' and orange gazanias.

● Combine yellow flowers with golden or green-and-gold leaves for a warm and sunny planting. Try *Coreopsis grandiflora* 'Calypso' with the shrubby honeysuckle *Lonicera nitida* 'Lemon Beauty'.

tip . . .
Make a harmonious colour scheme look even more striking by choosing flowers in very similar shades, but with differing shapes, such as globes, daisies, spires and umbels. The closely related colour holds together the entire group while the varied shapes create visual interest.

harmonies with red

Hot and lively harmonies create high drama in the garden. Green foliage plays an immensely important role in a hot harmony by acting as a buffer among so many brightly coloured flowers, while yellow-green foliage introduces a lighter note.

● Dark reds marry well with purple or maroon, although it is best to restrict this powerful combination to a small scale to avoid too sombre a look. Try the chocolate plant, *Cosmos atrosanguineus*, with *Sedum* 'Purple Emperor'.

● Dusky purple leaves look wonderful with red if used in moderation, although gloomy in excess amounts. Try *Physocarpus opulifolius* 'Diabolo' as a backdrop for red dahlias.

● Clear red and bright orange positively sing with warmth and life. Try partnering orange lilies with bright red *Crocosmia* 'Lucifer'.

above: Sumptuous dark red chocolate cosmos (*Cosmos atrosanguineus*) is perfect against a green background.

above: Blue *Agapanthus* harmonizes well with purple and soft pink African daisies.

contrasts

Because of the way our eyes perceive a bright colour, we need to see it in conjunction with a complementary, contrasting colour in order for it to appear at its most intense. If a planting were composed solely of orange flowers, for example, the part of our eye that perceives the colour orange would soon start to tire and perform less well. However, pairing orange with its natural contrast, blue, will not only stimulate the eye but ensure that we see both colours at their most intense.

The most vivid contrasts are based on the primary colours of blue, yellow and red. However, there are many other possible contrasts that are a little less bold, such as lime-green with purple, scarlet with blue-green, and gold with indigo blue.

Colour contrasts are bright and powerful, and there is often reluctance to make up contrasting combinations for this reason.

right: Spires of magenta pink *Diascia* make a strong contrast with silver.

colour contrasts ...

... combine colours that are distinctly different
... are lively and stimulating
... can be strong and bright or soft and muted

above: Orange tulips are the ideal partner for the many blue spring bulbs.

contrasts with blue

The calming effect of blue makes its contrasting colours look hotter and even more intense.

● Bright orange and deep or clear blue is one of the most vibrant contrasts that can be created. A little goes a long way, so start by using it in a small-scale planting. Try orange tulips with blue grape hyacinths (*Muscari*).

● Pale blue or mauve with apricot looks altogether softer and can be used on a larger scale. Try *Potentilla fruticosa* 'Daydawn' with a lavender such as *Lavandula angustifolia* 'Munstead'.

● Lime-green makes an unusual and stylish contrast, particularly with clear, deep blue. Try *Eucomis bicolor* (pineapple flower) with *Nigella damascena* (love-in-a-mist).

contrasts with yellow

Yellow creates a sparkling and lively contrast to the cooler colours on the other side of the colour wheel.

● Purple and gold makes a sumptuous contrast that can easily look over-rich without plenty of foliage. Try *Geranium phaeum* with the golden grass *Milium effusum* 'Aureum' and golden-leaved hostas.

● Clear blue and bright yellow make an immensely pleasing combination. Try golden dogwood, *Cornus alba* 'Aurea' underplanted with bog sage (*Salvia uliginosa*).

● Yellow is very effective at lightening dark green, which is especially useful in shade. Try drifts of yellow daffodils around and under heavyweight evergreens such as *Mahonia* and *Prunus lusitanica* (Portuguese laurel).

above: Blue *Myosotis* contrasts with yellow primroses and *Euphorbia polychroma*.

contrasts with red

The intensely dramatic nature of red makes it the most powerful of all colours to use in making up colour contrasts.

● Red with green is the easiest contrast to create. Although these two look very striking together, the natural predominance of green has an immensely calming effect. Try scarlet pelargoniums against a dark evergreen hedge, or *Tropaeolum speciosum* (flame creeper) or the brilliant autumn foliage of Virginia creeper (*Parthenocissus quinquefolia*) threaded across a large conifer.

● White makes a sparkling contrast to red flowers. Try pure white *Sutera* 'Blizzard' with scarlet pelargoniums.

● Red flowers with yellow foliage is sunny and uplifting. Try *Lychnis chalcedonica* with a yellow bamboo like *Pleioblastus auricomus*.

above: Red dahlias stand out well against a background of green foliage.

buffer colours

Although colourful flowers and dramatic foliage plants are undeniably the stars of the garden, they would have far less appeal without an attractive **backdrop** of **neutral shades** to act as a foil. These neutrals – foliage plants and those with white or cream flowers – are the hard-working **backroom** boys of the garden. Their function is to **moderate** and **separate** the effects of the stronger colours. Buffer colours come into their own in summer most of all, when the sheer range and strength of flower colours in the garden can become almost overwhelming.

While the majority of flowering plants have their own built-in **complementary** foliage, many of the newer garden hybrids of annual bedding plants have been bred for maximum flowers on a compact plant. So little leaf is visible that there is no natural buffer colour at all, so unless you want an unbroken carpet of colour such plants need to be mixed with plenty of **foliage plants**.

far left: Use foliage as a buffer between bright flowers. Here *Miscanthus* grass breaks up *Rudbeckia* and *Aster*.

left: Purple foliage brings drama to a border, harmonizing with red and contrasting with white.

below: An abundance of soft yellow *Verbascum* acts as a foil for darker shades.

foliage

Green, the predominant colour of nature, is calm and soothing, making the perfect foil to almost all planting schemes. On a garden-wide scale, green is the best colour to choose for hedges and trees, rather than gold or purple, which can create a jarring, rather artificial note. Within a border, be sure to incorporate several evergreens of the boring-but-useful school, such as *Prunus lusitanica*, *Viburnum davidii* and a wealth of different conifers.

Their value as foundation plants will soon become clear, breaking up potentially indigestible groups of bright colours and becoming invaluable in winter when there is little else of interest. For summer and autumn, ornamental grasses such as *Calamagrostis* and *Miscanthus sinensis* varieties dance with life and movement.

Grey and silver make superb buffers to a wide range of colours, either cooling and calming with bright shades or harmonizing with soft pastels. Few of these plants are bold eye-catchers in their own right, which makes them all the more useful when used as mixers with other plants.

Gold and purple foliage introduce a more dramatic note into a planting and are rarely suitable to use as buffer colours unless they tone in with a scheme that is deliberately hot and upbeat, such as red or orange flowers. Much more amenable are plants with leaves that are primarily green but suffused with tints of colour, such as the yellow-green leaves of several hostas or the slight red flush of *Cotinus coggygria*.

flowers

As well as foliage, flowers can be used as buffers. White is outstandingly useful but it is brilliant and light-reflecting, which means that large flowers are attention-seeking in their own right. When looking for buffers for a planting, choose smaller flowers, particularly tiny ones like *Crambe cordifolia* or *Gypsophila paniculata* that form a haze of little blooms.

Relatively few flowers are pure white; many are subtly tinted with a shade of another colour, giving blush-white, ivory and cream. These make much easier companions in a border than pure white.

Look carefully at white flowers and you will see that many have markings of another colour, such as the green tints of *Clematis* viticella 'Alba Luxurians' or the pink flushes on *Lilium regale*. Use these as a guide when choosing which whites to use as buffers. The crimson-blotched white flowers of many cistus, for example, look marvellous among dark red flowers, the purple staining on the blooms of *Philadelphus* 'Belle Etoile' with purple flowers, and the golden central florets of white argyranthemums will allow them to mix particularly well with yellow flowers. Picking up on these echoes will help to create a truly harmonious and relaxing colour scheme.

your garden palette

yellow

yellow...

...is the colour of sunshine
...adds sparkle to a planting
...looks joyful and welcoming
...can lighten a gloomy spot

The colour of **warmth** and sunshine, yellow is the most cheerful of colours and brings a **light-hearted** touch to the garden. As well as an abundance of flowers from spring to autumn, there are a few yellow flowers to be found even in winter. Add in a plentiful selection of yellow and gold-variegated foliage (see page 64), and you will see that there is certainly no shortage of plants in sunny colours. While the brighter, brassy golds look at their best in **sunshine**, soft yellows can be used to bring warmth to shadier spots. No wonder it is many people's **favourite** colour.

Harmonies can be soft, sunny and appealing where paler shades are used, or more heated and **lively** in association with warmer colours. Contrasts are vivid, creating an immensely pleasing effect without being too bold. As the most abundant flower colour, it is easy to end up with a vast number of different yellows that sit uneasily together. Try to limit the number of shades used in a single planting.

right: *Helianthus annuus.*

using yellow with...

blue

A classic colour contrast that has plenty of 'bite' yet is still easy on the eye. Under the calming influence of tranquil blue, yellow develops an air of elegance that goes well in many parts of the garden.

try ...

Yellow narcissi with blue hyacinths. The two outstanding colours of spring, yellow and blue can be found in a great many bulbs. For a really striking display, plant narcissi and hyacinths in separate, identical containers – maybe three of each – and group them together when in flower. Grow in sun or part shade.

taking it further ...

Any more bright colours would water down the power of the contrast. However, white narcissi or tulips would add a refreshing note.

top: *Clematis viticella* 'Etoile Violette'.
above: *Lonicera nitida* 'Baggesen's Gold'.

top: *Potentilla fruticosa.*
above: *Achillea* 'Moonshine'.

top: *Hyacinthus orientalis* 'Delft Blue'.
above: *Narcissus obvallaris.*

purple

Regal purples and golds create the most luminous and opulent of colour combinations. Warm and very definitely theatrical, this is a partnership to use sparingly and with care.

try ...

A purple clematis such as *Clematis viticella* 'Etoile Violette' with a gold-foliaged host – a medium-sized conifer or a shrub like *Lonicera nitida* 'Baggesen's Gold'. The large, velvety, clematis flowers make a superb contrast of colour, shape and texture. Make sure the clematis you choose is a good, rich colour; the effect will be lost if it is too pale. Large, established plants make wonderful hosts for suitable climbers, and *Clematis viticella* varieties are eminently suitable as they can be cut down in autumn to reveal the evergreen for the winter months.

taking it further ...

Such a rich combination needs little embellishment. A skirt of a *Heuchera* hybrid with soft purple foliage can be massed around the host plant to further emphasize the contrast. Coppery reds can be introduced in late summer and autumn.

yellow

An all-gold planting of yellow flowers and foliage creates a long-lasting feeling of warmth and sunshine. The theatrical, less natural appearance of such a planting makes it a good one to site close to the house or in an enclosed area of garden.

try ...

Achillea 'Moonshine' with a yellow-flowered shrubby *Potentilla fruticosa* such as 'Katherine Dykes', best in full sun. Using distinct flower shapes is the key to success with very similar shades, and here the large, flat heads of achillea contrast well with the small buttercup-like potentilla blooms and ferny foliage.

taking it further ...

Gold-and-green foliage gives plenty of brightness, while the green introduces a more natural note. Golden privet (*Ligustrum ovalifolium* 'Aureum') is an easy and versatile shrub that lends itself to trimming into all sorts of formal shapes, to give structure as well as colour.

mix & match

left: *Kerria japonica* 'Pleniflora'.

spring top 5

1 **Forsythia** Popular it may be and some will say over-planted, but masses of egg-yolk yellow blooms are undeniably cheering after a long, gloomy winter. Remember to prune hard straight after flowering to keep straggly growth within bounds.

2 **Kerria** The yellow-orange 'pompon' blooms of the double-flowered *K. japonica* 'Pleniflora' are always to be relied upon. Although deciduous, the shrub's stems remain a fresh green all year and so do their bit for winter interest.

3 **Mahonia** Racemes or clusters of bright yellow flowers appear from mid-winter onwards, with the added bonus of a lovely fragrance. The leathery, thorny leaves make a splendid architectural display all year.

4 **Narcissus** Daffodils and spring are inseparable and there is an infinite number of yellows to choose from. The smaller flowers last the longest and often have a lovely scent, too. Choose varieties that flower at different times to have blooms all through the season – perhaps the aptly named 'February Gold' followed by bright yellow 'Little Witch' and lemon yellow 'Pipit'.

5 **Tulipa** Glowing yellow tulips such as 'Golden Apeldoorn' and 'Georgette' bring spring to a close with a glorious flourish of colour. Their tall stems give plenty of space to allow for a contrasting carpet of bedding plants beneath.

add blue

Ceanothus A breathtaking sight when covered with masses of powder-puff blooms in an amazingly intense shade of blue, ceanothus looks even more beautiful against yellow as a contrast. Grow against a warm wall in cold areas.

Clematis alpina and **macropetala** **varieties** Less vigorous than many species clematis, these two can be grown through shrubs and small trees – try 'Francis Rivis' or 'Pamela Jackman' through a golden forsythia.

Hosta Search out varieties of hosta with gorgeous blue-green foliage, such as 'Big Daddy' or 'Halcyon', to brighten shady spots, particularly as this colour is rare among shade-loving plants.

Also: blue varieties of lilac (*Syringa vulgaris*) and glaucous grasses.

add white

Aquilegia A favourite cottage-garden flower, columbines are utterly charming. Use the white varieties to lighten part-shaded spots under trees and large plants, where they will dapple the ground like large flakes of snow.

Chaenomeles speciosa 'Nivalis' Saucer-shaped flowers look all the more striking for being borne on the naked stems before the leaves appear. The white blooms stand out to perfection against a dark brick wall or a fence, and will lighten a shady spot as well as a sunny site.

Hyacinthus Often overlooked in favour of colourful varieties, white hyacinths have a subtle charm that the others lack. Grow them with yellow narcissi for a truly refreshing combination.

Also: *Exochorda* x *macrantha* 'The Bride' and many narcissi.

summer top 5

1 **Anthemis tinctoria** Basking in a sunny site, this ferny-leaved perennial bears large yellow daisies for many weeks.

2 **Bidens ferulifolia** This versatile frost-tender trailer bears numerous golden-yellow daisy flowers from early summer to the first frosts. Grow this vigorous sun-lover in hanging baskets, window boxes, as ground cover or tumbling down from a raised bed.

3 **Coreopsis verticulata** Go for gold with masses of bright flowers borne above feathery foliage.

4 **Heliopsis 'Loraine Sunshine'** A double-value perennial with green and white variegated foliage and large yellow daisies on tall stems.

5 **Rosa** Yellow roses can be found in abundance, in every shade from pale lemon to rich old gold, with only yellow rambler roses in very short supply.

left: *Coreopsis verticulata.*

left: *Potentilla fruticosa.*

add blue

Cerinthe major 'Purpurascens' Pop in small groups of this unusual annual to make an extra, eye-catching splash of colour with its blue bracts and glaucous foliage. It can self-seed freely, which is either a blessing or a curse depending on your style of gardening.

Eryngium Rounded heads of blue flowers with showy bracts make a marvellous contrast of shape as well as colour to the many yellow 'daisy' flowers of summer.

Viola Never forget the contribution that can be made by little plants at ground level. The dainty 'faces' of violas are particularly charming, and lovely for containers too.

Also: many clematis and campanulas.

add yellow

Helichrysum petiolare 'Limelight' Yellow flowers harmonize superbly with the rounded lime-yellow leaves of this floppy frost-tender perennial that grows well in borders or containers.

Origanum vulgare 'Aureum' Excellent ground cover or edging, golden marjoram is bright yellow in sun and greeny-gold in part shade. And you can eat it too!

Phormium 'Yellow Wave' The sword-shaped leaves of New Zealand flax make it an architectural eye-catcher for a border or container. The yellow-edged green leaves of this variety look marvellous against a dark background. Show off its shape to the full with a surround of low-growing plants.

Also: golden-variegated foliage (see page 64) and grasses such as *Hakonechloa macra* 'Aureola' (see page 65).

autumn top 5

1 Clematis tangutica The golden lanterns of *C. tangutica* are borne for many weeks, the later ones nestling among the fluffy seed-heads from earlier blooms. Do grow it where the flowers can be seen against the sky – on an arch, pergola or obelisk.

2 Heliopsis Tough, easy perennials, the golden daisies of 'ox-eyes' create a long-lasting show. Rather like sunflowers in appearance, the blooms are showy, double or semi-double in form. Stake tall varieties in early summer to make sure of a good display into autumn.

3 Phygelius aequalis 'Yellow Trumpet' Create an exotic look with these tall stems clad with numerous tubular, pale yellow flowers. Encourage taller growth by placing this plant with its back to a wall or fence, or plant out in the border and treat like a perennial.

4 Hypericum 'Hidcote' Rose of Sharon is almost too easy to grow. In late summer the saucer-shaped flowers almost cover the foliage, turning the shrub into a golden dome.

5 Potentilla fruticosa These undemanding shrubs bear masses of five-petalled flowers for months, well into autumn. However, they are less than lovely in winter, so do not place in a prime position.

add purple

Aster Michaelmas daisies and autumn go hand in hand. One of the loveliest is *Aster* x *frikartii* 'Mönch', which is also much more resistant to the mildew that plagues many varieties. Beloved by butterflies too.

Rosa The sumptuous blooms of purple roses can be truly superb and repeat-flowering varieties such as 'Falstaff' and 'The Prince' will continue to perform into autumn. Add in fragrance and you have a heavenly flower.

Sedum 'Purple Emperor' Bold, flat heads of tiny flowers and rounded clumps of purple-flushed foliage make this a superb front-of-the-border plant to provide a contrast of colour and shape.

Also: purple-foliage shrubs (see page 68) and *Geranium* 'Chocolate Candy'.

add red

Acer palmatum The scarlet autumn tints of the Japanese maples look absolutely glorious if placed where the foliage is backlit by the sun.

Chrysanthemum Rich, rusty reds of chrysanthemums mingle with golden late-flowering perennials to make an end-of-season pageant of colour. Compact varieties such as the Yoder chrysanthemums are excellent for containers.

Monarda 'Cambridge Scarlet' Tubular flowers of bergamot, also known as bee balm for its popularity with bees, have a fringed, almost fluffy appearance. Borne on tall stems, they make a dramatic border display.

Also: cannas and penstemons.

blue

blue...

... is cool and soothing
... can be used to create depth
... mixes well with many colours
... creates an air of tranquillity

Approachable and adaptable, blue is a great favourite in the garden and could also be described as one of the most sociable colours. Blue really thrives on companionship, as without contrast it can look flat and boring. The range of shades is infinitely variable too, from soft silver blues and lavenders through enchanting sky blues to deep azure, and there is a broad choice of plants. There is an abundance of blue flowers from early spring to late summer, while autumn brings rich lavenders and some startling electric blues. Very little blue can be found in winter, which is just as well, as the chilly nature of this colour would not be welcome during the coldest months.

Harmonies and pale pastel schemes with blue are easily used to excess because it is such a safe colour to work with. Injecting some bold colour can make all the difference. However, be wary of blue with red or purple as the combination can be dull and lifeless.

right: *Iris reticulata.*

using blue with...

gold

Blue and yellow makes an invaluable combination in any garden, but more richness and contrast comes from using the deeper purple-blues and glowing golds. These darker shades look most at home late in the season when nature's colours take on correspondingly richer tints.

Try ...
Thuja occidentalis 'Rheingold' with a dark blue-purple clematis such as 'Perle d'Azur' scrambling through it. The conifer's old-gold colouring remains unflagging all year round and the clematis gives an extra garnish of summer blooms that contrast in shape, texture and colour with the conifer. Grow them in either sun or part shade.

Taking it further ...
Purple foliage adds a touch of drama, and is a little less flamboyant than if purple flowers were to be used, as well as being much longer lasting. Decorative vegetables like beet and chard are showy and unusual.

top: *Santolina pinnata* subsp. *neapolitana* 'Sulphurea'.
above: *Geranium* 'Rozanne'.

silver

Blue flowers against silver foliage look absolutely marvellous, the silver being close enough in colour to blue to pick out some of the colouring, yet different enough to make a handsome backdrop. Several blue-flowered plants, including lavender and perovskia, combine the two and are great value.

Try ...
One of the many good blue hardy geraniums with *Santolina pinnata* subsp. *neapolitana*. The large blue saucers of a spreading geranium plant make an exquisite contrast to the silver, finely cut santolina foliage (this variety is one of the daintiest) and both enjoy full sun.

Taking it further ...
Pink completes a classic combination that is a firm favourite. Pinks (*Dianthus*) offer a wide range of varieties – 'Doris' is a popular and reliable one – and are beautifully scented.

above left: *Clematis* 'Perle d'Azur'.
left: *Thuja occidentalis* 'Rheingold'.

top: *Hydrangea macrophylla* 'Mariesii Perfecta'.
above: *Cornus controversa* 'Variegata'.

white

Marrying blue and white is crisp and refreshing, marvellous for lightening a shady spot. As well as flowers, bring in foliage that is sharply marked with white for long-lasting interest.

Try ...
One of the many blue hydrangeas such as *H. macrophylla* 'Mariesii Perfecta' with the variegated wedding cake tree, *Cornus controversa* 'Variegata'. While the hydrangea forms a rounded bush with mop-headed flowers, the cornus develops a dramatic tiered structure clothed with green-and-white leaves. Both do well in shade, though acid soil is needed for the hydrangea flowers to remain blue rather than change to pinky mauve.

Taking it further ...
Fresh greens look enchanting in a woodland situation and hardy ferns look completely at home. *Dryopteris filix-mas* looks good from spring to autumn and is tolerant of a wide range of situations.

left: *Muscari aremeniacum.*

spring top 5

1 *Aquilegia* The most delightful blues belong to Fl hybrids, with much larger blooms that their old-fashioned cousins. Look for 'Blue Bird' (clear blue with a white centre), the darker 'Blue Jay', and 'Adonis Blue', which is sky blue with long spurs.

2 *Clematis alpina* and *macropetala* varieties Bring a touch of heavenly blue to the garden with these easy and amenable climbers that are tolerant of shade and exposure. Single or double, the nodding bells are equally appealing and they are ideal for arches, pergolas and trellis, and even for growing in a large container.

3 *Iris sibirica* Late in the season, as the other spring blues die away, these elegant, slender irises open their intricately marked blooms. They look particularly stunning near water, but unlike most irises, will happily grow almost anywhere.

4 *Muscari armeniacum* Grape hyacinths spread themselves rapidly to form a carpet of fresh green, grass-like leaves, making a lovely backdrop to the azure-blue flower cones.

5 *Pulmonaria* A superb perennial, with many varieties having exceptionally deep blue flowers – 'Mawson's Blue' is a good choice. Lungworts are tolerant of shade, so they are excellent under large shrubs like lavatera that don't fill out until later on.

blue and white

Amelanchier lamarckii The snowy mespilus is aptly named when smothered in panicles of white flowers, and it looks glorious when underplanted with a spreading carpet of blue aquilegia or muscari.

Lunaria annua var. albiflora The white form of honesty is far lovelier than the more frequently found purple. This is a charming cottage-garden plant for lightening the gloom beneath trees and large shrubs.

Viburnum x juddii Not only do the good-sized rounded heads of white flowers look tremendous, but they have a fabulous perfume too. This rounded shrub gives space for underplanting with ground cover as well.

Also: Spiraea 'Arguta' (see page 141) and spring bulbs.

blue and green

Acanthus spinosus The huge, dark green leaves of acanthus are perfect for bringing a touch of drama to a shady spot. The deeply divided leaves form a sizeable mound and in a congenial spot this is a perennial that will soon spread.

Angelica archangelica Most imposing of the herbs, angelica forms a large clump of fresh-looking leaves through which shoot immensely tall, bright green stems topped from late spring and through summer with spectacular greenish-white flowerheads.

Epimedium Epimediums make superb ground cover for retentive soil in shade. The delicate, heart-shaped leaves make a carpet of fresh green sometimes tinted with red. Cut back the old leaves in late winter so as not to detract from the new growth.

Also: many hostas and ferns.

summer top 5

1 *Abutilon x suntense* 'Jermyns' Sun and shelter are essential for this tall shrub. Give it the best spot in the garden and enjoy the masses of blue-mauve flowers that look like a flock of exotic butterflies come to rest.

2 *Agapanthus* The blue African lily bears tall stems topped with enormous round heads of small trumpets. Enchanting with low-growing silvery plants such as *Stachys byzantina* and *Artemisia* 'Powis Castle'.

3 *Clematis – large-flowered hybrids* Blue clematis abound in summer, with plate-sized flowers in every shade from palest lavender to clear china blue to deep blue-purple. Ensure a decent display by planting in deep, fertile, retentive but well-drained soil, with the top growth in the sun and the roots in the shade.

4 *Lavandula* An essential plant for lovers of fragrant flowers and foliage, lavender is superb for edging and makes an amenable companion to a vast range of other plants.

5 *Nigella damascena* Short-lived this hardy annual may be, but the beauty of love-in-a-mist makes it always worthy of inclusion. Large blue flowers – deep blue in the case of 'Miss Jekyll' – surrounded by a ruff of green float on top of feathery foliage.

left: *Ceratostigma willmottianum.*

blue and silver

Eucalyptus gunnii Spare the secateurs and spoil the plant, for to enjoy the most silvery, rounded foliage from the cider gum calls for drastic pruning every spring. This will ensure that you have a spectacular shrub to grace the back of a sunny border.

Helichrysum petiolare A tender perennial that is widely grown in containers, the branching, horizontal stems clad with silvery leaves are great in borders, too, and make a handsome contrast to rounded and spiky-shaped plants.

Pyrus salicifolia 'Pendula' With narrow silver leaves and a weeping habit, this is a lovely tree for the back of a large border or in a none-too-prominent spot in a lawn where its untidy winter shape can go unnoticed.

Also: silver-leaved annuals such as *Senecio cineraria* 'Silver Dust' and silver-blue conifers.

blue and pink

Cistus 'Silver Pink' While many of the sun roses are bold and brash in flower, the colour of this variety is described by its name – a soft pearly pink that fades to almost white in the centre.

Erigeron karvinskianus Only grow the Mexican daisy if you are a lover of informal gardens, for it will rapidly self-seed in borders, walls and between paving slabs. The dainty pale pink daisies keep flowering throughout the summer months.

Lavatera 'Blushing Bride' Invaluable for rapid growth, this variety of tree mallow has flowers of palest pink against soft green-grey foliage. An excellent shrub that is likely to flower all summer until halted by the frosts.

Also: roses and diascias.

left: *Nigella damascena.*

autumn top 5

1 **Clematis 'Perle d'Azur'** There is an ever-increasing choice of late-flowering clematis in all shades of blue, but 'Perle d'Azur' is a particular old favourite, with sky-blue blooms as lovely as its name.

2 **Ceratostigma willmottianum** Flowers of such a piercing blue are unusual so late in the season (probably only the gentian rivals it). Shrubby plumbago makes an unforgettable late-season display and looks looks stunning among autumn foliage with its own leaves developing brilliant tints too.

3 **Hibiscus syracius 'Oiseau Bleu'** Late to get going in spring, this sun-loving shrub more than makes up for it at the back end of the season with masses of large, purple-centred, blue-mauve blooms that have more than a touch of the exotic.

4 **Passiflora caerulea** The passion flower bears its curiously shaped blue and white flowers all summer and well into autumn. Given a long hot summer, the late blooms will nestle among bright orange egg-shaped fruits.

5 **Teucrium fruticans** A self-contained colour combination, with soft blue flowers set against silvery green foliage. Grow against a wall for the best display.

blue and gold

Helenium 'Butterpat' These rich golden daisy blooms borne on strong, tall stems look tremendous behind low plants such as ceratostigma or autumn-flowering ceanothus.

Sambucus racemosa 'Plumosa Aurea' Fast and easy to grow, the golden elder benefits from annual spring pruning and a dressing of fertilizer high in potash to be sure of non-stop display of golden fringes of foliage.

Spiraea x bumalda 'Goldflame' Plant at the front of the border for a mound of deep orange-gold foliage. For a paler shade opt for 'Gold Mound' or 'Golden Princess'.

Also: *Choisya ternata* 'Sundance' (see page 133) and many conifers.

blue and purple

Heuchera These make excellent foliage perennials for border edges and for containers, where you can appreciate the attractively wavy-edged leaves. Purple varieties are many and include 'Chocolate Ruffles', 'Palace Purple', and 'Plum Puddin'.

Phormium tenax The spiky-leaved New Zealand flaxes are renowned for their dramatic foliage. Create dark contrasts with purple varieties such as *P. t.* 'Atropurpureum' or the smaller *P.t.* 'Bronze Baby'.

Saxifraga 'Black Ruby' This saxifrage forms a neat little mound of dark purple, frilly-edged leaves, perfect for border edges out of full sun. A pretty contrast with pale blue campanulas.

Also: *Sedum telephium* subsp. *maximum* 'Atropurpureum' and *Viola riviniana* Purpurea Group (see page 141).

orange

... is bold and uncompromising
... brings warmth to a planting
... creates a lively atmosphere
... stands out in strong sunlight

Redolent of blazing summer days and the fiery displays of autumn, orange flowers shout for attention. True orange occurs in comparatively few flowers, which makes plant selection more straightforward by narrowing the range available – when creating colour contrasts, take care not to stray into salmon or dark orangey-yellow, which would have much less impact. Many of the best orange shades come from annuals or tender perennials, so experiment with these seasonal flowers first before committing to long-lasting perennials and shrubs.

Contrasting combinations of orange with just one other colour are supremely effective. Harmonies with other warm colours need more care but can be tremendously successful in the right place. The sheer uncompromising nature of orange often makes gardeners reluctant to use it, but stick to simple combinations to ensure that its full beauty and power will be revealed.

right: *Rosa* 'Whisky'.

using orange with...

top: *Euphorbia chariacas* subsp. *wulfenii*.
above: *Erysimum* x *allionii*.

lime green

This unusual yet ultra-smart pairing is guaranteed to impress. The lime tones down the orange just a little, creating a colour combination that is just the right side of lurid.

Try ...
Wallflowers (*Erysimum*) with *Euphorbia chariacas* subsp. *wulfenii*. Euphorbias offer the best selection of lime 'flowers' (the colouring actually comes from bracts rather than true flowers), and this variety forms bold, architectural heads that will complement the soft, 'painted velvet' of the wallflowers to create an attractive spring combination for sun or very light shade.

Taking it further ...
Yellow links both colours and creates a greater feeling of warmth. The large yellow daisies of *Doronicum grandiflorum* 'Miss Mason' (leopard's bane) are striking yet easy to grow.

yellow

The citrus shades of lemon and orange give a zesty, exciting combination. Partnered with such a bright colour, orange seems to become much less forthright without losing its impact. For the best effects, choose clear lemon yellow rather than paler creams or darker golds.

Try ...
Euphorbia griffithii 'Dixter' with Welsh poppies (*Meconopsis cambrica*). Both these perennials flower in late spring to early summer, the euphorbia forming a large, bold clump while Welsh poppies produce simple, dancing blooms on short stems. The poppy self-seeds abundantly to create an enchanting effect in sun or partial shade.

Taking it further ...
Blue contrasts well with both colours but should be used sparingly, and with plenty of green foliage in between as a buffer. Forget-me-not (*Myosotis sylvatica*) is an easily grown biennial that flowers at the same time.

top: *Meconopsis cambrica*.
above: *Euphorbia griffithii* 'Dixter'.

top: *Felicia amelloides*.
above: *Mimulus aurantiacus*.

blue

A sophisticated but friendly combination, particularly when these two colours are used alone with only foliage as a buffer. There are many variations: clear blue looks stunning, while lavender and mauve also look very handsome. Orange-flowered plants in blue-glazed pots look terrific too.

Try ...
Mimulus aurantiacus (shrubby musk) with *Felicia amelloides* (blue marguerite). The rich orange musk flowers make a glorious contrast to the little blue daisies of the marguerite. Both are long-flowering, frost-tender plants, ideal for sunny summer pots or borders.

Taking it further ...
Stick to simplicity – adding any other colour would water down the effect.

left: *Tulipa* lily-flowered group.

spring top 5

1 *Berberis darwinii* A tough evergreen shrub that is transformed in spring by a profuse clusters of tiny deep orange flowers.

2 *Berberis linearifolia* **'Orange King'** A less dense shrub than *B. darwinii* and not quite so hardy, but its show of flowers has even more impact. Most of the many berberis have flowers in the yellow-orange-red range, but they vary greatly in tone and some can be difficult to place. Their autumn berries also vary in colour, which may help you choose.

3 *Erysimum* Wallflowers, with their cheery little velvet flowers, mix well with other spring blooms. *E. x allionii* and *E. chieri.* 'Orange Bedder' have glowing orange flowers.

4 *Euphorbia griffithii* **'Dixter'** In late spring this euphorbia looks from a distance as though its stem tips are on fire as its flower bracts turn a flaming orange.

5 *Tulipa* Tulips offer some of the best opportunities for lively colour schemes. Among the early flowerers is the short, stripy-leaved 'Princesse Charmante'. Later, 'Generaal de Wet', 'Orange Favourite' and 'Orange Monarch' are all striking. Many varieties combine orange with other shades, such as the plum-flushed 'Prinses Irene', for example, which can be the starting point for an interesting colour scheme.

orange and lime or apple green

Euphorbia myrsinites A euphorbia with typical heads of lime-green bracts, but these appear at the end of short floppy stems clothed in fleshy leaves that make this little plant look rather like a succulent.

Helleborus argutifolius Wonderfully imposing in spring when large clusters of apple-green flowers are borne against a background of grey-green leaves.

Tulipa **'Spring Green'** A lovely late tulip with broad flames of apple green marking its creamy white petals.

Also: other hellebores and euphorbias.

orange and yellow

Euphorbia polychroma Rounded and bushy, this has the brightest yellow bracts among euphorbias; they last well and age to a limy yellow-green.

Forsythia The ubiquitous forsythia can by turns be cheerful or brassy, depending on its setting. Choose an equally bold orange companion and plenty of green buffer foliage. *F. suspensa* is a more graceful shrub with softer colouring than many other forsythias.

Primula veris If you have a sunny spot that is not too dry, then carpet it with cowslips. The delightful soft yellow flowers should not be overpowered by a complex planting, but they would shine in the foreground of a hedge of berberis or a distant cloud of euphorbia.

Also: golden grasses and, of course, narcissi.

summer top 5

1 *Calendula* Pot marigolds were once simple orange daisies, but are now available in a wide range of orange, gold and copper tones, both single and double.

2 *Crocosmia x crocosmiiflora* **'Emily McKenzie'** A medium-sized crocosmia with a dark red-brown throat to its vivid orange flowers, striking against the fresh green sword-like leaves.

3 *Eschscholzia* **'Orange King'** The Californian poppy is a rewarding annual, its orange almost glistening in the sunshine. Give it a hot dry home and pair it with other sunshine colours.

4 *Lilium* Lilies come in many tones of orange from flushed salmon to coral. Among the excellent true oranges are 'Fire King', 'Enchantment' and 'Jetfire', and the tiger lily, *L. tigrinum splendens*, with blooms like Japanese lanterns.

5 *Mimulus aurantiacus* In a warm, sheltered spot this delightful little shrub will flourish, and be covered all summer with apricot flowers like large snapdragons. Ideal for containers too.

left: *Lilium* 'Enchantment'.

left: *Dahlia* 'Weveric'.

orange and blue

Clematis Among the large-flowered clematis at this time of year are a number of beautiful blue varieties. 'Perle d'Azur', 'Lasurstern' and 'William Kennet' are all tried and tested favourites. 'Haku Okan' has a lovely dark blue double flower. *C.* x *eriostemon*, with navy blue, spidery flowers, has a leaning, rather than twining habit, which makes it ideal for weaving through a host shrub.

Nigella hispanica A love-in-the-mist with flowers of a rich, deep blue. Planted en masse they create a hazy effect that makes a magical contrast when grown with more solid orange and gold flowers.

Salvia patens A world away from the dumpy scarlet annuals used in a million formal bedding schemes, *S. patens* makes a graceful, airy plant with beaky-looking flowers the colour of a Mediterranean sky.

Also: *Felicia amelloides* (see page 135) and tradescantias (see page 141).

orange and lime green

Bupleurum fruticosum When the glossy dark evergreen leaves of this wall shrub become covered in countless round heads of yellow-green flowers, it would form an ideal background for many bold, fiery-coloured flowers that also enjoy the sun.

Molucella laevis This very distinctive annual, beloved of flower arrangers, has the common name of bells of Ireland, which precisely describes its tall spires of green flowers.

Nicotiana langsdorfii A tall tobacco plant with flowers that hang from the multiple stems like miniature pixie hoods. It's a good mixer with hot colours, either as an occasional punctuation mark for contrast or, in a large drift, as a creamy green buffer.

Also: the more familiar tobacco plant, *Nicotiana alata*, and *Alchemilla mollis* (see page 132).

autumn top 5

1 **Campsis radicans 'Indian Summer'** In a warm corner, this is a vigorous, almost thuggish climber, treasured for its large, exotic-looking blooms – it is sometimes called the trumpet honeysuckle or trumpet vine.

2 **Dahlia** Dahlias come in a good range of oranges. Those suffused with more than one shade, like a tropical sunset, are especially eye-catching. 'David Howard' is a startling but immensely effective combination of single orange flowers paired with dark bronze foliage.

3 **Eccremocarpus scaber** The Chilean glory flower may not survive the winter, but it is a fast grower, soon covered with short spikes of flame-coloured little tubular flowers.

4 **Potentilla fruticosa 'Tangerine'** Potentillas are such useful shrubs, and the buttercup-like flowers of 'Tangerine' are a clear, soft orange, which is not washed out yet not at all strident.

5 **Pyracantha 'Saphyr Orange'** Not for nothing are pyracanthas called firethorns – with the ripening of their innumerable clusters of berries they will set a wall ablaze.

orange and yellow

Cotinus coggygria 'Golden Spirit' A form of the popular smoke bush that, by contrast to the more familiar varieties, has leaves that are washed through with soft gold. Lovely towards the back of a border.

Luzula sylvatica 'Hohe Tatra' A golden woodrush which seems equally happy in the damp or dry and, rewardingly, just gets brighter and brighter as the days shorten and darken.

Rudbeckia fulgida Black-eyed Susans are fail-safe perennials that make a sunny border explode with colour just when you think the garden is slowing down. Rich yellow petals make a startling contrast to their prominent chocolate-brown eyes.

Also: *Sambucus racemosa* 'Plumosa Aurea' (see page 140) and other golden-leaved shrubs.

orange and blue

Ageratum These powder puffs in soft mauve-blue mix well with orange in many forms. While many varieties are neat and bun-shaped, popular for edging, the tall growth of 'Blue Bouquet' looks more at home rubbing shoulders with other plants.

Caryopteris clandonensis 'Heavenly Blue' A particularly beautiful combination of flower and foliage: countless cockades clear blue of tubular flowers are set among the dainty grey-green leaves.

Ceanothus 'Autumnal Blue' Unlike most of its spring-flowering cousins, this variety of Californian lilac bears its powder-puff clusters of blue flowers late in the year. Glossy green foliage makes a stalwart contrast to the ever-changing autumn colours that abound.

Also: *Ceratostigma willmottianum* and many clematis, both climbing and herbaceous kinds.

purple

Few flower colours are as **exotic** as the **rich** plums and velvety, **regal** purples that fall within this part of the spectrum. The number of flower varieties available in these colours has been steadily increasing, and those who like a challenge will enjoy the thrill of building up a collection. Many of the best dark flowers are annuals, with some perennials and climbers, but only a few shrubs. There are, however, a number of shrubs with **stunning** purple foliage.

Harmonies with these dark colours can be **stylish** but they can also be glowering and dark if not handled with care. Contrasts, on the other hand, can provide startling and very **sophisticated** effects.

right: *Salvia nemerosa* 'Ostfriesland'.

purple...

... cools down hot colours
... adds richness to a planting
... adds a sense of space and tranquillity
... can bring interest to a shady corner

using purple with...

lime-green or cream

Sophisticated without being harsh, this combination uses two quite unusual colour groups in a way that is sure to impress gardeners and non-gardeners alike.

Try ...
Clematis 'Jackmannii' with *Clematis viticella* 'Alba Luxurians'. These two clematis both flower in late summer but are very different, the one with rich purple blooms, the other with smaller, creamy white petals tipped green that flutter in the slightest breeze.

Taking it further ...
Adding blues or blue-mauves would create a new dimension. The scrambling blue *Geranium wallichianum* 'Buxton's Variety' would run well around the feet of these climbers and its white eye would echo the white clematis above.

top: *Clematis viticella* 'Alba Luxurians'.
above: *Clematis* 'Jackmannii'.

top: *Cynara cardunculus*.
above: *Tulipa* 'Queen of Night'.

silver

This is a wonderful combination, radiating an atmosphere of sophisticated cool. It is also perhaps the easiest to achieve, as there are plenty of silver-foliaged plants to choose from. Purple foliage is rarely dark enough to achieve the best effect, so this is the place for those really deep purple flowers.

Try ...
Tulipa 'Queen of Night' set against the young foliage of the cardoon or giant artichoke (*Cynara cardunculus*). The cardoon's new leaves are very silver, almost blue-silver in some lights, while the tulip is virtually black. They make a good combination for a sunny spot in late spring.

Taking it further ...
Adding any other colour would knock back the power of the contrast, but a little blue, such as a sprinkling of forget-me-nots (*Myosotis sylvatica*), would work.

blue

Dark purples with blue are less of a shock, more a complementing of the unusual with the familiar – it is like an extreme version of a traditional pastel colour combination with the intensity turned up.

Try ...
Dark roses with blue geraniums: team the shrub rose 'Tuscany Superb' with *Geranium* x *magnificum* and they will flower together in early summer and suit a semi-shaded spot.

Taking it further ...
Such a combination makes a good high point for a pastel border. Adding paler and less emphatic pinks, blues and mauves takes little away from a powerful combination like this, but continues the theme.

top: *Geranium* x *magnificum*.
above: *Rosa* 'Tuscany Superb'.

mix & match

left: *Crocus* 'Remembrance'.

spring top 5

1 *Akebia quinata* Few climbers provide such fresh-looking foliage so early in the season, and the vivid green makes a lovely backdrop to dark purple-red blooms. Shelter is needed to avoid late frosts doing their worst.

2 *Berberis thunbergii* **'Red Chief'** Startlingly deep-coloured leaves can be used to make a striking contrast to numerous spring bulbs, particularly as the arching branches are excellent for showing off the tall stems of daffodils and tulips.

3 *Crocus* Many of these easy spring beauties have globes of gleaming, rich purple flowers.

4 *Sambucus nigra* **'Black Beauty'** The dark purple leaves of this elder look lovely with a skirt of pale spring bulbs beneath. Later, clusters of pinky purple flowers create a self-contained harmony.

5 *Viola riviniana* **Purpurea Group** Colour contrasts can work right down to the smallest plant, and little clumps of the purple-leaved violet will thrive almost anywhere, even in dry shade.

purple and lime green

Alchemilla mollis An easy plant for ground cover and edging. Its scallop-edged lime-green leaves look handsome in their own right and in early summer the plant erupts into a froth of lime-yellow flowers.

Helleborus foetidus Despite its name, this evergreen hellebore does not stink! Its long-lasting pale green bells open early in spring, and each has the thinnest rim of purple, which will provide a subtle tie to red or purple neighbours.

***Milium effusum* 'Aureum'** Bowles' golden grass, a broad-leaved grass that's easy to grow and easy to place. Its colour lasts all year, clear sunny yellow in good light or more limy in deeper shade.

Also: epimediums and euphorbias.

purple and blue

Ajuga reptans Easy and excellent ground cover with spires of blue flowers above a carpet of glossy foliage. Grow the purple-leaved 'Atropurpurea' to intensify this colour partnership even further.

Brunnera macrophylla The deep blue perennial forget-me-not is happy in shade, so grow it beneath purple-leaved shrubs where its blooms twinkle through the dark foliage.

Scilla sibirica Heavenly deep blue flowers pop up as if from nowhere from this little spring bulb. Scatter it in a whole carpet – once you've grown ten, think what a hundred or two hundred would look like.

Also: forget-me-nots (*Myosotis sylvatica*) and many lungworts (*Pulmonaria*).

summer top 5

1 *Acanthus spinosus* Acanthus flowers are actually white, but it is the tall stems of showy purple bracts that catch the eye. Somewhat like a stiff foxglove, it is similarly tolerant of shade. Wonderful with *Clematis viticella* 'Etoile Violette' behind.

2 *Clematis* Royal purple blooms look marvellous threading through other plants. In good soil and shelter, grow one of the large-flowered hybrids with plate-sized blooms. In less than perfect situations, opt for a *Clematis viticella* cultivar, such as 'Polish Spirit' or 'Etoile Violette', which are altogether tougher.

3 *Digitalis purpurea* The tall spires of foxgloves soar above their neighbours for just a short while in summer.

4 *Persicaria microcephala* **'Red Dragon'** A stunner! On the leaves, borne on wide-arching stems, dark purple mingles with burgundy and mint green, with silver chevron markings. Makes a very unusual container plant as well as offering something quite different for the border.

5 *Rosa* Purple roses abound in summer, mainly on old-fashioned shrub roses and their modern-day look-alikes: the sumptuous deep purple 'Cardinal Richelieu', soft purple 'Reine des Violettes', crimson-tinted 'Mme Isaac Pereire' and the soft blackberry rambler 'Veilchenblau'. Browse through a rose catalogue to see more of the vast range of shades available.

purple and blue

Ipomoea tricolor 'Heavenly Blue' An annual climber that is well worth the necessary cosseting early in its life to enjoy a fabulous display of huge, sky-blue trumpets. It is perfect for eliminating any potentially sombre atmosphere created by lots of purple.

Delphinium Aristocrats of the herbaceous border, the tall spires of blue delphiniums are more than worth the spring battle with slugs, who also adore them. Great for introducing a vertical element, too.

Salvia uliginosa Clusters of deep, sky-blue flowers borne on slender stems wave gracefully in the air – not the tidiest of perennials, but one of the loveliest.

Also: *Salvia patens* (see page 140) and *Penstemon heterophyllus* (see page 139).

purple and pale pink

Geranium x oxonianum 'Wargrave Pink' Great ground cover or border edging, with sprawling foliage and masses of soft pink flowers all summer.

Lavatera 'Barnsley' The reddish 'eye' in the centre of these pale pink, hollyhock-like blooms helps to bridge the gap between pink and purple.

Verbena 'Silver Anne' Graceful frost-tender perennial with a lax, spreading habit that makes it a lovely plant for containers and border edging, where its large heads of bright pink flowers can be fully appreciated.

Also: beauty bush (*Kolkwitzia amabilis*) and *Erigeron karvinskianus*.

left: *Digitalis purpurea.*

autumn top 5

1 **Clematis viticella 'Purpurea Plena Elegans'** Dainty little rosettes, crushed blackberry in colour, smother this easy climber in late summer. It makes a superb partner for larger, single flowers such as hibiscus or late single roses.

2 **Cotinus coggygria** Purple-leaved forms of the smoke bush, such as 'Royal Purple', look especially splendid when the richly coloured foliage becomes tinted with autumn shades and overlaid by the airy 'smoke puffs' of tiny flowers.

3 **Leycesteria formosa** The Himalayan honeysuckle is lightly tinted with purple throughout, from its tall straight stems and neat leaves to the dangling clusters of wine-purple berries within their papery bracts. Ideal where you want a hint of purple rather than a bold statement.

4 **Liriope muscari** Tussocks of lilyturf make a useful but unremarkable fringe to a path or border, so it is always a pleasant surprise to discover the flower stems – columns of tiny beads the colour of violets – emerging from the broad grass-like leaves.

5 **Verbena bonariensis** Tall, branched, 'see-through' stems topped with flat heads of blooms create an airy haze of purple – striking yet not overpowering.

purple and silver

Festuca glauca Neat little hedgehogs of intense silver-blue grass look lovely at the front of a border or in a container.

Santolina To be treasured for its filigree foliage rather than its yellow button flowers, so trim hard in spring and lightly in summer for a neat rounded mound. Finest and most silvery is *Santolina pinnata* subsp. *neapolitana*.

Stachys byzantina 'Silver Carpet' This low-growing, sun-loving perennial with woolly leaves that just cry out to be stroked, lives up to both its varietal name and its common name of lamb's ears.

Also: *Elaeagnus* 'Quicksilver' and other silver-variegated foliage (see page 72).

purple and white

Hibiscus syriacus 'William R. Smith' Although one of the latest shrubs into leaf, by the end of the summer this tall, upright shrub is smothered in large blooms that look tropical enough to attract hummingbirds. Their purity makes a startling contrast to purple.

Nicotiana sylvestris An astoundingly tall and imposing annual (perennial in very mild areas) this tobacco plant bears candelabras of long-necked, snow-white trumpet blooms above huge, paddle-shaped, fresh green leaves. It is also beautifully scented.

Physostegia virginiana 'Summer Snow' Neat and upright amid the lax abundance that characterizes the autumn garden, little clumps of white flowers shine brighter still among dark companions.

Also: *Hydrangea paniculata* 'Grandiflora' (see page 137) and white-flowered clematis.

white

White is not a colour in the true sense of the word, but has an inestimable effect in the garden: in hot sun it is cool and **refreshing**, in shade it is invaluable for **lightening** the gloom, and in the evening it is the last colour to remain visible long after the others have faded into the twilight. Many white flowers are also beautifully **scented**.

Harmonies with white are refreshing and **uplifting**, although a good background of foliage needs to be incorporated to avoid the effect being too restrained. The idea of an all-white border is attractive, but too much of a very pale colour can soon become dull. Unless your tastes lean heavily towards such ultra-cool colours, an all-white planting should only be created as one part of a larger garden. Used in a contrasting mix, white makes an excellent **buffer** between bright shades (see page 18) as it does not react with any other colour. As well as white flowers, white-variegated foliage can be used to similar effect.

right: *Magnolia stellata.*

white...

... is crisp and refreshing
... looks smart and sophisticated
... is tranquil and serene
... catches the last evening light

using white with...

top: *Geranium psilostemon*.
above: *Anthemis punctata* subsp. *cupaniana*.

pink

Loud magenta pinks can be hard to place in a planting as they have a nasty tendency to shout at their neighbours. Of course, there is no such problem with amenable white, which calms down its potentially violent partner.

Try ...
Geranium psilostemon with *Anthemis punctata* subsp. *cupaniana*. The statuesque and striking magenta-flowered geranium is complemented by the white daisy flowers and feathery grey anthemis foliage. Grow in full sun.

Taking it further ...
Silver cools the bright pink even further and adds a touch of sophistication. *Lychnis coronaria* 'Alba' combines the best of both worlds – silver-grey foliage with white flowers.

green

White is never lovelier and more refreshing than when seen against a mass of green – snowdrops, cherry blossom, water lilies all delight the senses in their own seasons. While green abounds at every time of year, spring is when all foliage is at its peak. Plant pools of white flowers and pale leaves among the copious fresh green foliage of grasses, perennials and ferns.

Try ...
White-edged hostas such as *Hosta* 'Albomarginata' with pools or drifts of *Narcissus* 'Thalia'. A lovely spring partnership for part or full shade.

Taking it further ...
Blue flowers always contrast marvellously with white and green. The carpet-forming lesser periwinkle (*Vinca minor*) has deep blue flowers and glossy foliage.

top: *Hosta* 'Albomarginata'.
above: *Narcissus* 'Thalia'.

top: *Waldsteinia ternata*.
above: *Dicentra spectabilis* 'Alba'.

yellow

A blend of white and yellow creates a happy, light-hearted combination that is especially good for lightening gloomy corners where the sun seldom reaches.

Try ...
Dicentra spectabilis 'Alba' (bleeding heart) with *Waldsteinia ternata*. The dicentra's flowers are unusual, like little white hearts dangling from the arching stems. Below, the shining green foliage of the mat-forming waldsteinia is scattered all spring with equally shining saucers of yellow flowers.

Taking it further ...
Rich green foliage throws the light flowers into relief and emphasizes their fragile beauty. A large-leaved shrub like *Fatsia japonica* makes a striking contrast of shape as well as colour.

mix & match

left: *Viburnum* x *burkwoodii.*

spring top 5

1 *Chaenomeles speciosa* **'Nivalis'**
Flowering quince or japonica is one of those shrubs that needs discipline – train it against a dark wall or fence so that the white flowers, like large buttercups, really stand out.

2 *Erica carnea* Carpets of pure white winter-flowering heathers such as 'Springwood White' look like fallen snow, wonderful against the dark-coloured foliage that can dominate the garden in winter. Unlike many other heathers, *E. carnea* is tolerant of some lime.

3 *Iberis sempervirens* **'Schneeflocke'**
Perennial candytuft is an old cottage-garden favourite and deservedly so, with masses of pure white flowers on a carpet of rich green foliage.

4 *Prunus avium* **'Plena'** Place the double-flowered form of the wild cherry against a dark background – holly, for example, or yew – and be stunned by a magnificent display of spring blossom.

5 *Viburnum* The viburnums are a charming collection that can span the spring, starting with the remnants of the winter-flowering *V. tinus,* then moving on to delectably fragrant species such as *V.* x *burkwoodii, V.* x *carlcephalum* and *V.* x *juddii.*

white and white-variegated foliage

Aegopodium podagraria **'Variegata'** The very name of ground elder sends shivers down a gardener's spine, but this variegated variety is not so disastrously invasive and is immensely useful as groundcover or even lined along the edge of a path like a miniature hedge.

Arum italicum **'Marmoratum'** The arum's arrow-shaped leaves, with their bold creamy veining, look good for many months. This plant is charming for underplanting in shady sites and difficult corners.

Cornus alba **'Elegantissima'** Variegated dogwood is a tremendous all-year plant. Its green leaves widely edged with white making a refreshing background for bright flowers that last from spring to autumn. Its scarlet stems give a change to the scheme in winter.

Also: hostas and spotty-leaved lungworts such as *Pulmonaria saccharata* 'Argentea'.

white and blue

Chionodoxa lucillae A dainty blue, white-eyed bulb known as glory-of-the-snow because of its earliness to flower and resilience in bad weather. It makes a lovely partner for winter heathers.

Veronica peduncularis **'Georgia Blue'** Outstanding for ground cover and deserving to be more widely grown, this is rather like a very aristocratic speedwell, with masses of small, deep blue, white-eyed flowers. As a bonus, it is also evergreen.

Vinca minor Grow this vigorous, tough, ground-covering lesser periwinkle under trees and shrubs and on banks, to stud the gloom with clear blue flowers.

Also: *Scilla sibirica* (see page 140) and forget-me-nots (*Myosotis sylvatica,* see page 138).

summer top 5

1 *Cosmos* **'Purity'** A truly unbeatable annual, its tall, branching stems topped with large pure white blooms all season long . It is perfectly at home either mixed in a border of permanent plants or as part of a bedding scheme.

2 *Crambe cordifolia* An ideal buffer plant, crambe's great cabbage-like leaves do not prepare you for the delicacy of the myriad tiny flowers that form a billowing cloud above your head. Gypsophila provides a similar effect on a smaller scale.

3 *Lilium* Lilies not only look tremendous, but their perfume packs a real punch too. Plant them in pots near a sitting area, and choose several different species so the flowers span several months, starting with the pink-and-yellow-flushed *Lilium regale* and finishing with the Oriental hybrids.

4 *Philadelphus* The mock oranges are deservedly loved for their sweet scent, although the variety too often planted is the enormous 'Virginal'. Much more manageable in size is the double-flowered 'Manteau d'Hermine'.

5 *Rosa* There is a wealth of white roses to choose from, ranging from little ground-coverers such as 'Yorkshire' and floribundas like 'Margaret Merrill' and 'Princess of Wales' to rampant ramblers such as 'Rambling Rector'. Many 'white' roses have cream or blush tints, so choose carefully to fit your colour scheme.

left: *Philadelphus* 'Manteau d'Hermine'.

left: *Escallonia* 'Iveyi'.

white and pink

Diascia Little known until a few years ago, diascias have been 'discovered' for use in all sorts of places – hanging baskets, containers, raised beds and borders – where their gently spreading stems of bright flowers can trail downwards.

Osteospermum Sun-loving African daisies offer some marvellous shades of pink, often mixed with other colours. Excellent in containers as well as borders, and particularly handsome with other tender perennials.

Penstemon Tremendous long-flowerers, these evergreen perennials come in a huge range of varieties from pink-flushed 'Mother of Pearl' and soft 'Hidcote Pink' to rose pink 'Evelyn', so best to choose when in flower.

Also: a huge range of roses and geraniums.

white and silver

Cynara cardunculus Magnificent silver leaves of the stately cardoon harmonize beautifully with white flowers, with contrast provided by the deep blue tufted flowers on tall stems.

Hebe pinguifolia 'Pagei' Give borders a neat edge with this compact carpeting hebe, with little grey leaves all year round.

Helichrysum italicum subsp. serotinum People either love curry plant or hate it – not for its elegant silver-grey foliage, but because of its pungent scent that is strongest after rain. The little yellow flowers can be cut off if they do not suit your scheme.

Also: *Stachys byzantina* (see page 141) and artemisias (see page 132).

autumn top 5

1 *Anemone* x *hybrida* 'Honorine Jobert' Japanese anemones can become invasive, but all is forgiven when their tall stems are covered in saucer-shaped blooms.

2 *Escallonia* 'Iveyi' Bright glossy green foliage shows off large clusters of white flowers. An easy, vigorous shrub for the back of the border.

3 *Hydrangea paniculata* 'Grandiflora' Huge cone-shaped panicles of flowers literally weigh down the branches. Not altogether pure white, the pink-spotted blooms show off best against a background of purple foliage.

4 *Lilium* Late-blooming lilies include Oriental hybrids such as 'Kyoto' and the gold-striped 'Imperial Gold', and species like as the enormous golden-rayed lily, *L auratum platyphyllum*.

5 *Saxifraga fortunei* Starry panicles of flowers rise on wiry stems above scallop-edged leaves – handsome for border edges and useful in shade.

white and red

Cotoneaster horizontalis In autumn the unassuming herringbone cotoneaster looks as though someone has put a match to it – both leaves and berries turn bright, flaming red.

Fuchsia 'Mrs Popple' Crimson blooms with violet underskirts make a vibrant display on a hardy little shrub.

Potentilla fruticosa 'Red Ace' Masses of small, tomato-red flowers are produced for months. This is a shrub that needs neighbours of a contrasting shape to jazz up its indeterminate appearance.

Also: *Sedum* 'Autumn Joy' (see page 141) and red-berried shrubs such as *Berberis* 'Pirate King'.

white and yellow

Catalpa bignonoides 'Aurea' An outstanding foliage plant, its soft gold, heart-shaped leaves are best if the plant is hard pruned every spring rather than allowed to grow into a tree. Place at the back of the border or grow on its own as a specimen.

Fremontodendron 'California Glory' Turn a sunny wall to gold with the waxy-petalled blooms that are produced until the frosts arrive – a large wall, though, for it is a somewhat vigorous.

Phygelius aequalis 'Yellow Trumpet' A forest of tall stems clothed with many soft yellow trumpets brings an exotic touch to the border. Or let it poke up through a wall-trained *Cotoneaster horizontalis* for a striking contrast.

Also: some red hot pokers (*Kniphofia*) and golden-leaved evergreens (see page 64).

pink

pink...

... is warm and welcoming
... can be soft and relaxing
... cool pale pinks look best in soft morning light
... darker shades add richness and depth

The most diverse of all the colours in the garden, pink has infinite variety. Shades vary from **palest blush** through candy floss and warm **rose** to rich fuchsia and vivid **magenta**. Although considered to be an easy colour to use, this is not necessarily the case. Salmon-pinks are hard to partner with other plants, while loud shocking pinks need careful placing. Look closely at pink flowers: many are actually marked with another colour, such as a white centre or purple veining, and will give clues as to their favoured company.

Such is the range of shades that no single rule can be applied to all pinks. Many pinks contain some blue and these create **delightful harmonies** with blue, silver and white. Deep warm pinks, on the other hand, contrast well with soft yellow and lime-green. While paler shades are easy to combine with other colours, the temptation to play over-safe can result in a rather dull planting, so experiment with unusual combinations.

right: *Ageratum houstonianum.*

using pink with...

purple foliage

Vivid pinks make a dramatic contrast to purple leaves. The dark foliage is averted from any danger of becoming sombre by a succession of vibrant blooms.

Try ...
A glowing pink rose such as 'Gertrude Jekyll' or the gorgeously striped 'Ferdinand Pichard' with a backdrop of *Physocarpus opulifolius* 'Diabolo'. Shrub roses are the best choice to grow with other plants in a mixed border, and both the rose and the physocarpus will enjoy a sunny spot.

Taking it further ...
Underplant the rose with a skirt of purple-leaved heuchera, plus pink tulips to start off the season with a blaze of colour and *Schizostylis* 'Mrs Hegarty' to round off the year.

top: *Penstemon heterophyllus*.
above: *Cosmos bipinnatus* 'Daydream'.

top: *Diascia barberae* 'Ruby Field'.
above: *Verbena* 'Silver Anne'.

top: *Physocarpus opulifolius* 'Diabolo'.
above: *Rosa* 'Ferdinand Pichard'.

blue

Soft blush pinks and pale blues or mauves are a classic partnership that never fails to please.

Try ...
Cosmos bipinnatus 'Daydream' with *Penstemon heterophyllus*. A frost-tender annual, the cosmos bears large pale pink blooms that are strongly flushed darker pink, on tall stems clad with feathery, green foliage. It looks wonderful above the spreading blue-mauve penstemon, which flowers for a long time. Grow in full sun.

Taking it further ...
Silver foliage adds life to a sunny planting, but to avoid the combination becoming a little too insipid, inject a touch of drama by using the bold, jagged foliage of *Cynara cardunculus* (cardoon) as a background plant.

pink

Such is the range of shades and hues of pink that a single-colour planting can contain an enormous number of variations without looking in the least dull. The secret of success is to place different shades of pink carefully to mediate between the light and dark tones.

Try ...
Verbena 'Silver Anne' with *Diascia barberae* 'Ruby Field'. These trailing tender perennials will mingle their stems together to make a lovely combination of pale and rich pink. Great when grown in a container or the front of a border, in full sun.

Taking it further ...
Plants with pink tints in their foliage will accentuate the overall colour while also acting as buffers. Use *Cordyline australis* 'Albertii', its broad striped leaves edged with pink, as a bold centrepiece for the planting.

mix & match

spring top 5

1 *Camellia* x *williamsii* **'Donation'** Dozens of rich orchid-pink blooms appear quite early in the season. Camellias are not the easiest of plants to grow, needing shelter, dappled shade and neutral to acid soil, but 'Donation' is one of the most accommodating and well worth the effort.

2 *Clematis montana* **var. *rubens*** Give this rampant clematis plenty of room to scramble so that you can enjoy its cascades of pale pink blooms that almost cover the purple-flushed stems.

3 *Daphne mezereum* The upright stems of mezereon are wreathed with fragrant, brightly coloured blossoms. All parts of the plant, especially the red berries that follow, are toxic.

4 *Prunus incisa* **'Kojo-no-mai'** A true delight when the twisted branches of this small decorative cherry are wreathed in pale pink blossom. Ideal for a containers as well as in a border.

5 *Tulipa* Pinks tulips are often overlooked in favour of their numerous red and yellow cousins, but there are many beautiful varieties. A great choice is the bright lily-flowered 'China Pink', which look glorious above forget-me-nots or double daisies (*Bellis perennis*).

left: *Daphne mezereum*.

pink and white

Bergenia **'Silberlicht'** While pink varieties are more widely grown, the white form of this tough perennial contrasts best of all with its dark green leathery leaves that aptly earn it the name of elephant's ears.

Dicentra spectabilis **'Alba'** The little snow-white lockets of the white form of bleeding heart are very appealing and make a graceful spread beneath pink spring-flowering shrubs.

Syringa vulgaris **'Madame Lemoine'** Lilac's popularity never seems to fade. 'Madame Lemoine' is an old variety with, of course, the heavenly lilac scent.

Also: many other white-flowered shrubs, including *Viburnum* x *juddii* (see page 141) and *Spiraea* 'Arguta' (see page 141).

pink and blue

Camassia leichtlinii Every part of the camassia is narrow and delicate, from the tall, slender stems to the pointed starry flowers that come in all shades of blue. It prefers a damp sunny spot and looks very much at home in sparse long grass.

Myosotis sylvatica
Grow forget-me-nots on a large scale to carpet the ground with a haze of blue. They are wonderful grown under deciduous shrubs and tall bulbs like tulips.

Primula **'Miss Indigo'** A double-flowered primula which is intensely coloured and immensely charming, with small, deep blue blooms that are rather like miniature roses.

Also: *Brunnera macrophylla* (see page 133) and *Clematis alpina* and *macropetala* varieties (see page 133).

summer top 5

1 *Buddleja* **'Pink Delight'** Not only does this variety of butterfly bush have enormous racemes of bright pink flowers, but it brings a wealth of extra, ephemeral colour in the form of all the butterflies that flock to its nectar-rich flowers.

2 *Geranium psilostemon* Unlike most herbaceous geraniums, this one demands attention when its mass of vivid magenta-pink, black-centred blooms appear. It is classically paired with silver or white, but experiment with more unusual companion colours such as dark purple or even hot orange.

3 *Hebe* **'Great Orme'** Invaluable garden shrubs for a sunny spot, hebes flower for months on end and the blooms of 'Great Orme' are especially large and long-lasting.

4 *Lavatera olbia* A lavatera's flowers look rather like single hollyhocks set among the grey-green leaves. of this fast-growing shrub. They go on flowering for months and are becoming available in an increasing number of shades, from the original candy pink to palest apple-blossom and duo-tones (see page 137).

5 *Papaver orientale* **'Patty's Plum'** Subtlety is not something normally associated with the huge, brazen blooms of oriental poppies, but those of 'Patty's Plum' are a delightful crushed strawberry colour.

below: *Lavatera olbia*.

left: *Colchicum autumnale.*

pink and blue

Ceanothus thyrsiflorus 'Repens' Create a carpet of blue with this ground-covering form of the Californian lilac, which thrives in sun-baked situations and well-drained soil.

Lithodora diffusa 'Heavenly Blue' Small but heavenly, this little carpeting plant becomes a shimmering mass of incredibly deep blue flowers. Only for those on acid soil, alas.

Nepeta x faassenii The lax, spreading stems and cloudy blue flowers of catmint make it ideal for border edges, raised beds, and for the classic combination of underplanting for roses. As the name suggests, cats adore it.

Also: large-flowered clematis hybrids (see page 133) and hardy geraniums.

pink and silver

Ballota pseudodictamnus Ballota's comfortingly gentle woolliness look best when the lax stems are tumbling across a path or from a raised bed (well-drained soil is a must). Its soft silver green mixes well with all tones of pink, from pastel to puce.

Onopordum nervosum Silver, spiky and exceptionally imposing, the Scotch thistle should never be confused with its weedy cousin. It makes a dramatic statement in a pastel scheme and holds its own among other bold plants such as brilliant pink roses.

Salix elaeagnos Tall and graceful with long, slender, silver-grey leaves, this handsome willow is one of the few silver shrubs to grow in damp soil – most need a dry sunny spot.

Also: *Cynara cardunculus* (see page 134) and artemisias.

autumn top 5

1 Anemone x hybrida 'Queen Charlotte' Japanese anemones may be somewhat invasive, but all can be forgiven when their gorgeous, long-lasting blooms appear – this variety is a deep, glowing pink.

2 Colchicum autumnale 'Pleniflorum' Just as many plants are reaching the end of their season, up pop the bubblegum-pink colchicums, often mistakenly but understandably called autumn crocus. They are also known as naked ladies as the large pink goblet flowers appear without any supporting leaves.

3 Cyclamen hederifolium A small-scale charmer that, despite its tiny and delicate-looking blooms, is tough and reliable. It even grows in dry soil at the base of hedges and trees, where it creates carpets of pewter-grey marbled leaves through the summer.

4 Schizostylis 'Mrs Hegarty' The sugar-pink flowers of kaffir lilies, like miniature crocuses on branching stems, look like they should belong to the spring rather than the autumn palette, but they are produced in abundance long after most other flowers have come and gone.

5 Sedum 'Ruby Glow' Innumerable tiny flowers make up the flat heads of sedums and are beloved by bees. 'Ruby Glow' is a deep, dark pink variety with handsome, fleshy greenish-purple foliage.

pink and red

Berberis 'Pirate King' Nature really goes to town with its autumn colours, and this variety of berberis makes a self-contained colour pageant with deep crimson foliage and orange-red fruits.

Euonymus europaeus 'Red Cascade' Combine pink autumn flowers with the spindle bush and you will create a stunning colour shock, for its shiny red fruits split open to reveal orange seeds within.

Viburnum opulus 'Compactum' This compact variety of the bushy wayfaring tree is laden in autumn with large clusters of rich, sealing-wax red berries.

Also: many other red-berried shrubs, from the prostrate *Cotoneaster horizontalis* to the high-reaching *Pyracantha* 'Saphyr Rouge'.

pink and blue-mauve

Aster x frikartii 'Mönch' Most handsome and reliable of all the Michaelmas daisies, 'Mönch' carries its large lavender-blue, yellow-centred flowers on tall stems.

Clematis heracleifolia Not a climber, this, but a herbaceous clematis, with sweet-scented little starry flowers in blues that can vary from lavender to near-navy.

Eryngium x oliverianum An architectural perennial that adds both colour and shape, with oval heads of flowers that are sharply defined by a surround of spiky bracts, all suffused with a metallic blue.

Also: *Ceanothus* 'Autumnal Blue' and *Ceratostigma willmottianum.*

red

Hot and exciting, red is synonymous with danger and even aggression – think of phrases like 'seeing red' and 'a red rag to a bull'. But a red rose is also a token of love, and fiery hues bring passion and drama to a planting in a way that less powerful colours can never manage.

Unlike blues and greens, achieving a harmonious mix of reds can be tricky, but contrasts are nearly always dramatic and eye-catching. Foliage in shades of red blend together much more easily than flowers – just picture how autumn is set aflame with every possible hue from claret to copper juxtaposed with abandon.

Use red only very sparingly around patios and seating areas, or avoid it altogether, as this lively colour is not at all tranquil or relaxing. Red is perhaps the hardest colour to use in the garden, but get it right and the rewards can be tremendous.

right: *Persicaria* and *Dahlia* 'Bishop of Llandaff'.

red...

... is upbeat and exciting
... catches the eye and seeks attention
... looks best in bright sun
... is striking but challenging

using red with...

purple

A handsome and sophisticated combination. The secret of success is to use clear and dark red, as it mixes with other colours much better than more complex shades such as blood red and crimson, which can look muddy. Use plenty of purple foliage as well, to give sufficient body and background to the planting.

Try ...
Crocosmia 'Lucifer' with *Cotinus coggygria* 'Royal Purple' (smoke bush). This crocosmia's tall spikes of flower bells glow like devils' pokers from the fresh green swords of the leaves. With the round, damson purple foliage of the smoke bush they make a dramatic summer partnership for sun or very light shade.

Taking it further ...
Silver foliage adds sparkle. The filigree foliage of *Artemisia* 'Powis Castle' would be delightful in a sunny position.

top: *Cotinus coggygria* 'Royal Purple'.
above: *Crocosmia* 'Lucifer'.

top: *Choisya ternata*.
above: *Rosa* 'Flower Carpet Red Velvet'.

green

Green is red's natural contrast, sitting directly across the colour wheel. It's a familiar and appetizing association: a red flush on a green apple, tomatoes on a bed of lettuce. Rich and light greens, rather than dark or acid shades, usually produce the most pleasing combinations.

Try ...
Rosa 'Flower Carpet Red Velvet' with *Choisya ternata* (Mexican orange blossom) in a sunny situation. This groundcover rose bears velvety red flowers that contrast beautifully with the glossy lobed leaves of the choisya. This is an exceptionally long-lasting combination as the rose blooms for many months and the choisya is evergreen. As a bonus the choisya's sweetly scented white flowers appear just before those of the rose and you may get also some late summer blooms too.

Taking it further ...
Gold – not yellow – adds even more richness. *Rudbeckia* 'Golden Jubilee' is absolutely perfect as the golden daisy flowers have a dark red eye, pulling the trio together.

white

For a refreshing pairing, white provides a bright contrast that we enjoy all year – imagine snow on holly berries and cream on strawberries – but is often under-used in the garden.

Try ...
Leucanthemum vulgare (ox-eye daisy) with *Papaver rhoeas* (field poppy). These simple flowers, once thought of as cornfield weeds, have an individual charm. Put them together to enhance each other, the scarlet poppies brightening the white daisies and the daisies emphasizing the fragility of the poppy petals. Both are easy-to-grow annuals perfect for a summer meadow garden in poor soil and sun.

Taking it further ...
Chrysanthemum segetum (corn marigold) is a cornfield annual for the same conditions. Its sunny colour make a rich harmony with red and also picks up the daisies' yellow eyes.

top: *Leucanthemum vulgare*.
above: *Papaver rhoeas*.

spring top 5

1 *Acer palmatum* Maples are renowned for their autumn colour, but the unfurling spring leaves of purple or red-leaved varieties such as 'Burgundy Lace' are also brilliantly coloured.

2 *Chaenomeles* x *superba* 'Crimson & Gold' Most varieties of this tough, easy-to-please shrub (often called japonica) are pink or white, but this is a true red, further enhanced by a furry mass of bright gold stamens. As a bonus, the new growth is also shot through with red.

3 *Rhododendron* Few spring-flowering shrubs have greater impact than rhododendrons in full bloom. 'Elizabeth' and 'May Day' are both popular rich red varieties, and 'Scarlet Wonder' is ideal for a container or a small garden.

4 *Ribes speciosum* Akin to a fuchsia in its appearance, the clear red blooms of this easy shrub dangle gracefully beneath arching branches.

5 *Tulipa* There is a multitude of red tulips to choose from, from the low-growing 'Red Riding Hood' with its purple-mottled foliage to the multi-headed *T. praestans* 'Fusilier', the aptly named ramrod 'Grenadier' and the untamed curls of 'Red Parrot'.

red and white

Exochorda x *macrantha* 'The Bride' A star shrub that becomes entirely clothed in glistening, round-petalled white flowers in late spring. The arching branches of the plant give it added grace.

Narcissus Creamy white daffodils mix more easily than some of their brassier yellow sisters. 'Mount Hood' and 'Finlandia' are large, sturdy varieties, while the late-flowering *N. poeticus* 'Pheasant's Eye' has a tiny red-orange cup that could be picked up by nearby tulips or emerging bronze foliage.

Spiraea 'Arguta' A reliable background shrub, this spiraea becomes a cascade of tiny confetti-like flowers in mid-spring, earning its name of bridal wreath.

Also: other white spring bulbs such as tulips, crocuses and snowflakes (*Leucojum*).

red and green

Asplenium scolopendrium Although the hart's tongue fern keeps its fronds through the winter, it is in spring that it really comes into its own. The new season's tongues, shining fresh and green as they erupt through the old foliage, bring life to shady ground beneath shrubs and trees.

Euphorbia amygdaloides var. *robbiae* With its undemanding nature, this euphorbia will quickly spread without growing too tall, making it invaluable as a buffer between bright colours. The airy heads of lime-green flowers make a good foil to more solid flowers.

Hosta Marvellous perennials with large, lush leaves. Popular all-green varieties include 'Royal Standard' with heart-shaped leaves, and *H. venusta*, with wavy edges.

Also: *Alchemilla mollis* (see page 132) and *Fatsia japonica* (see page 135).

summer top 5

1 *Canna* With their enormous leaves and flowers like bright jungle birds, cannas are becoming ever more popular for tropical-style plantings. Bright red varieties include 'Brilliant', 'Endeavour' and 'Roi Humbert'.

2 *Clematis viticella* 'Madame Julia Correvon' Most *Clematis viticella* varieties fall in the purple/mauve/white range, but 'Madame Julia Correvon's wide open flowers are a rich scarlet. An easy climber, it looks good scrambling up into trees and over arbours.

3 *Crocosmia* 'Lucifer' A large stand of 'Lucifer' is a fine sight, its clump of tall, grass green leaves topped by dozens of flower stalks, each with a row of brilliant red blooms like miniature trumpets ranged along the edge.

4 *Papaver orientale* As spring rolls into summer the crepe-paper petals of herbaceous poppies unfurl into shining saucers each with a black central blotch. Despite the 'oriental' in the name and the silken brilliance of the petals, even the most vivid, such as 'Beauty of Livermere', fit a cottage garden scheme better than an exotic setting.

5 *Rosa* Red roses come in all shades, from the clear, light cherry of 'Alexander' to the rich burgundy of 'Guinée' and 'Tradescant' and vivid orange-red 'Oklahoma'.

red and purple

Cordyline australis 'Black Tower' The cordyline's fountain of long, strappy leaves give it the appearance of a miniature palm tree. It is reasonably hardy in mild areas and makes a great partner for cannas and other exotics.

Lathyrus odoratus 'Matucana' A velvety purple sweet pea, 'Matucana' has a wonderful scent and mixes happily with other climbers: it would look tremendous weaving up a pillar with a scarlet, unscented rose.

Physocarpus opulifolius 'Diabolo' A useful backdrop or buffer shrub rather than one to take centre stage. The pale pink flowers are pretty seen close up, but it is the dark purple foliage that is so valuable for offsetting brilliant red or magenta flowers.

red and silver

Artemisia, especially 'Powis Castle' An immensely useful low shrub that fits into almost any planting as long as it is in a dry sunny spot. The feathery aromatic foliage is a terrific foil for every shade of red, especially the dark blood-clot hues that need a sharp, light contrast.

Elaeagnus 'Quicksilver' Fast-growing and extremely hardy, the silver foliage of this tall and elegant deciduous shrub looks particularly fresh and lovely in spring and summer.

Salvia argentea A very distinctive plant, this is one to go for if you are looking for something brilliantly silver with more impact than *Stachys byzantina* (see page 141) but more approachable than Scotch thistle (*Onorpoum nervosum* see page 139). The huge furry leaves mark it out from its shrubby cousins.

Also: silver-blue grasses such as *Festuca glauca* (see page 135) and many cistus varieties.

autumn top 5

1 **Cosmos atrosanguineus** The flowers of the chocolate plant are extraordinary – like large buttercups but in a real deep chocolate that can look dark red in some lights and almost black in others. And on a warm day they give off a chocolate scent. Needs careful placing against a light background.

2 **Dahlia 'Bishop of Llandaff'** Among the very large-flowered dahlias, the flower is all, but this sought-after smaller version is a perfect and unusual pairing of flower and foliage: single flowers of the clearest true red among dark purple leaves.

3 **Pelargonium** Often erroneously called geraniums, pelargoniums have long been a favourite choice for containers (and seem to fill every window box in the Swiss Alps). They are easy, fast-growing and colourful, and any of the many red varieties would be effective as a real attention-catcher.

4 **Penstemon** Penstemons, with their spikes of flowers like small foxgloves, seem to gain in popularity with every passing year. Most veer towards the pink or mauve part of the spectrum, but 'King George' is a rich scarlet, and 'Garnet' more claret-coloured.

5 **Schizostylis coccinea 'Major'** The kaffir lily's pretty flowers appear astonishingly late in the season, fragile cups of pointed petals among neat clumps of fresh green leaf blades. 'Major' is a good wine-red variety.

red and green

Fargesia murieliae A handsome, easily grown bamboo that soon forms a very tall, rustling background against which red flowers or foliage would show up well.

Ferula communis The giant fennel will grow taller than a man but its feathery foliage is so fine that it is best to think of it as a 'see-through' plant. It looks great with a hedge of copper beech behind it.

Musa basjoo A banana: the ultimate in an exotic planting! Massive, paddle-shaped, vivid green leaves are borne in an upright clump. Plant in a sheltered spot to avoid the foliage become wind-bruised and tatty.

Also: *Fatsia japonica* (see page 135) and *Tiarella* 'Mint Chocolate', for its purple-splashed leaves.

red and gold

Choisya ternata 'Sundance' Evergold rather than evergreen, this is a yellow-leaved variety of the Mexican orange blossom.

Hemerocallis 'Golden Zebra' A delightful little day lily with green-and-gold striped foliage as well as yellow flowers. Each bloom lasts only for one day, hence the name, but in such profusion that the plant gives weeks of colour.

Thuja occidentalis 'Rheingold' A dwarf conifer that forms a dense golden cone. It looks good all year, providing a useful addition to different seasonal colour schemes.

Also: heleniums and *Cornus alba* 'Aurea' (see page 134).

colourful foliage

foundation

Successful colour planting is all about creating partnerships. Some of the freest-flowering plants have the least interesting foliage, so a marriage with a **complementary** foliage colour creates the best of both worlds. All too often leaves are seen as poor relations to flowers, with their more immediate and entrancing beauty, but flowers without a balancing foil of foliage would be a sorry sight indeed. Foliage is the **foundation** on which almost any successful colour scheme should be built. Looking good at least from spring to autumn, and all year in the case of evergreens, the sheer **length of performance** makes foliage essential to any planting. A **tapestry** of leaves not only creates marvellous contrasts of colour to other flowering and foliage plants, but contributes much understated yet invaluable interest by way of shape and texture too.

top tips for successful foliage planting

● Use plenty of green as a buffer between flowers as well as plants with coloured foliage.

● Gold and purple leaves look striking but artificial, so use these in moderation to avoid an unnatural appearance.

● Variegated plants are attractive but avoid putting different variegations next to each other as their individual impact would then be greatly watered down.

● Combine different plant and leaf shapes and textures, for long-lasting interest.

● Choose the right plant for the right place. Most silver and grey-leaved plants, for example, need plenty of sun to thrive, while nearly all plants with large, soft leaves wilt in hot, dry sites.

above: This medley of leaf vegetables shows that edible plants can be grown for their looks, as well as to eat.

a glorious variety

Take a close look at foliage and see what a wonderful selection of colours is at your disposal. Once you have been amazed by the sheer depth and variety of greens, look at all the sparkling silvers, glaucous blue-greens, rich bronzes and golds, glowing reds, smoky purples, and a few plants whose leaves are so dark that they appear almost black. Then there are leaves with quite 'unleaf-like' colouring, such as *Actinidia kolomikta*, a relation of the kiwi vine, which looks as if its leaves have been dipped in white and pink paint.

Leaves vary in size and shape from the fine filigree of artemisias and the slender blades of ornamental grasses, to the large glossy hands of the castor oil plant (*Fatsia japonica*) and the deeply veined umbrellas of the gunnera.

Texture adds yet another facet to a planting. Soft-textured foliage is irresistible to the touch and such plants are lovely close to paths and patios, like the woolly leaves of *Stachys lanata* (lamb's ears) or the shaggy mop of the little conifer *Chamaecyparis pisifera* 'Filifera Aurea'. Texture affects our perception of colour too. The light-reflecting gloss of camellia or holly leaves gives them a different quality of colour from their mat-surfaced neighbours.

With many plants the effect of their foliage comes from the sum of the parts – it is not the individual leaves that are interesting, but the mass effect. These play a vital role in creating a background for flowering plants. Certain types of foliage have personality, presenting a bold overall shape or spectacular leaves. These are often called architectural plants

The golden rule with foliage is to plant all things in moderation. For example, lots of nondescript shapes would create a singularly average planting, but a few large-leaved plants like *Macleaya cordata*, *Fatsia japonica* and *Viburnum rhytidophyllum* work like visual 'full stops', creating a touch of drama and encouraging the eye to rest and take stock. However, a planting where large-leaved plants are in the majority would be just too restless and overdramatic.

evergreen versus deciduous

Evergreens are real stalwarts, invaluable in winter when there is little else to look at. But such reliable, hard-working plants are inevitably rather staid and unchanging in appearance. Come spring, there is nothing to compare with the brilliant vitality of all manner of burgeoning foliage, full of life and changing dramatically week by week. Both types of plant contribute greatly to the long-lasting good looks of a garden but neither should outweigh the other. Aim for a good balance: a useful rule of thumb is that evergreens should make up no more than a third of all the medium-sized to large plants in a border.

above: Plants provide an astonishing range of leaf shapes and colours.

'double whammy' plants

Plants that combine colourful foliage *and* flowers can make fabulous self-contained colour combinations – they are great in any garden but especially effective where planting space is limited. The best ones are exciting, and their long-lasting good looks mean they are tremendous value:

Golden foliage with blue flowers: *Caryopteris* x *clandonensis* 'Worcester Gold', *Tradescantia* 'Sweet Kate', *Vinca minor* 'Illumination'

Green-and-yellow foliage with yellow flowers: *Coreopsis grandiflora* 'Calypso'

Purple foliage with lime-green flowers: *Euphorbia dulcis* 'Chameleon'

Green-and-gold foliage with white flowers: *Gaura lindheimeri* 'Corrie's Gold'

Green, cream and white striped leaves with blue flowers: *Iris pallida* 'Variegata'

Hybridizing has also created some unhappy colours matches too: *Dicentra spectabilis* 'Gold Heart, *Phygelius* x *rectus* 'Sunshine' and *Weigela* 'Briant Rubidor' all have yellow leaves that clash with their pink flowers.

left: Contrasting foliage can be as bright and decorative as any flower.

greens

The most abundant of nature's colours, green is often thought of as a neutral in the garden. Yet there is a limitless selection of different shades, from pale lime-greens and apple tints through bottle and olive greens to the richest, darkest evergreens. Compare the sharp, acid green of new fern fronds caught in spring sunlight with the glossy emerald of a waterlily leaf; picture the sombre shades of yews and holly against the fresh green of grass. Tints of other colours join forces with green too, either washed through the leaves as in the blue-tinted glaucous greens, or subtly marked with another colour. Cool, gentle and refreshing, the invaluable contribution that all these different shades of green make to the garden should never be underestimated.

colour, texture and shape

A wonderful quality of greens is that, unlike other colours in the garden, they can be used extensively on their own with great success.

Colour can never be seen in isolation and is always influenced by other factors. This is never more true than with green, where the shape, form and texture of the leaves play a vital role in their appearance. While most delicate and large-leaved foliage plants dislike hot, dry conditions, they are absolutely perfect for shady sites under trees and large shrubs. Spring is their real season of glory, when leaves unfurl in so many delicate shades of fresh perfection, but they continue to look attractive for many months.

lush woodland effects

Among the best plants for a woodland setting are hardy ferns. The male fern (*Dryopteris filix-mas*) and the ostrich fern (*Matteucia struthopteris*) form tall stands, and Asplenium and Athyrium species are low and spreading. Epimediums form spreading clumps of rounded leaves tinged with bronze or red in spring, and lady's mantle (*Alchemilla mollis*) forms low clumps of scalloped-edged leaves.

If you are truly lacking in space you could even create a miniature forest floor planting in a large container, placed in a shady position and with soil that retains plenty of moisture.

star combinations

As the foundation colour of the garden, green looks good with almost everything but there are times when it becomes truly outstanding:

● Rich green with red or white flowers

● Dark blue-green with silver foliage and blue flowers

● Apple greens with white or cream flowers

● Dark green with golden foliage

● Lime-green contrasted with blue or orange, as a softer contrast with yellow, or harmonizing with pastels such as apricot or mauve.

above: The fingered leaves of an *Acer* (Japanese maple) are wonderfully delicate in shape as well as colour.

right: The tall stems of *Euphorbia characias* subsp. *wulfeni* provide year-round interest.

above: The scalloped leaves of *Alchemilla mollis* (lady's mantle) hold moisture in tiny quicksilver pearls.

colourful foliage 55

left: The huge glossy leaves of *Fatsia japonica* are invaluable for architectural effect.

above: Bamboo creates a jungle-like background in an exotic foliage planting.

right: A close look at the jagged leaves of *Melianthus major* reveals the sheer beauty of foliage.

top 10 green foliage plants

1 *Alchemilla mollis* The rounded clumps of soft green formed by lady's mantle make a pretty groundcover that lasts most of the year. After rain the leaves literally sparkle, when the scalloped edges remain rimmed with raindrops, like a beaded necklace.

2 *Choisya ternata* A shrub that never looks tired, the Mexican orange blossoms's smart oval leaves stay a glossy, rich green all year, with new spring growth the colour of grass.

3 *Dryopteris filix-mas* A hardy deciduous fern which is a delight as it unfurls its fresh green croziers in early spring, and for the rest of the season is an invaluable background green anywhere shady.

4 *Fargesia murieliae* An evergreen bamboo that quickly forms a tall stand of green canes topped with long green leaves. Invaluable as a backdrop to tropical-style planting or as a vertical accent to contrast with large round leaves and plants that grow outwards rather than upwards.

5 *Fatsia japonica* Like the choisya, fatsias provide a glossy green presence all year, but these are altogether more tropical-looking, with large, light-green leaves like broad hands. One for a shady, sheltered spot.

6 *Geranium renardii* The leaves of this geranium are little scalloped plates of grey green, with a soft, dimpled texture that makes you want to stroke them. As a bonus they turn a brilliant orange-scarlet in autumn.

7 *Helleborus argutifolius* This hellebore's leaves are strong and leathery, with a slight greyish cast. Its spiny edges don't encourage you to touch, but it makes a good contrast with softer, 'greener' greens.

8 *Melianthus major* A star choice for beautiful foliage if you have the room and can give it sufficient protection from hard frosts. The enormous arching, sage green leaves are deeply dissected and each leaflet is serrated, giving it a feathery look despite its size. The overall effect is of softness and elegance.

9 *Soleirolia soleirolii* There couldn't be a greater contrast between melianthus and this minute creeper, mind-your-own-business. Its tiny round leaves mass together in a bright evergreen cushion that from a distance looks like moss.

10 *Viburnum davidii* Out of flower most viburnums are very much background shrubs, but the distinctive ribs on *V. davidii*'s leathery leaves add invaluable textural interest.

greys, blues and silvers

The beauty of these pale-foliaged plants is subtle, perhaps less immediately obvious than other foliage colours, but their retiring nature makes them tremendously good companion plants. Indeed, for the true beauty of these ghostly shades to come shining through, they need to be in good company. Although rarely having enough personality to hold the attention for more than a few seconds, add some colourful flowers and a dramatic change takes place, with both groups of plants becoming far more beautiful when seen in relief against the other. Greys, silvers and blues are invaluable buffers for toning down hectic colours as well as being excellent for enhancing softer shades. Use these soft shades in a small garden to create an illusion of space.

shades of silver

Most of this very useful group of plants look best in summer. Although many are evergreen, during winter they become rather tatty and bedraggled. For the most part, grey and silver-foliaged plants thrive in sun and on free-draining soil, for their pale appearance is the result of having evolved to cope with drought. Look at the leaves and you'll see that much of the colouring comes from a coating of hairs or wax, which reduces water loss and protects the leaves from strong sunlight. Leaves which are finely divided to give a filigree appearance have evolved for the same reason.

While leaves are their principal attraction, many foliage plants also bear flowers. In some cases they are insignificant, as with artemisias and silver-leaved hebes. Other plants are much more showy, The airy blue-mauve flower stems of *Perovskia*, like lavenders, add greatly to the beauty of the whole plant, but with some plants the blooms can detract from their appearance. Trimming silver santolinas regularly to remove the button-shaped sulphur-yellow flowers will encourage plenty of fresh filigree foliage, and many gardeners remove the yellow daisies of senecios (*Brachyglottis*).

Very few silverlings thrive in moist soil, but one of the loveliest is a graceful shrubby willow, *Salix exigua*. It will do well in any but dry soil, but it loves a waterside situation. Some grey conifers such as *Chamaecyparis pisifera* 'Boulevard' and *Juniperus virginiana* 'Grey Owl' also like a good loamy soil that doesn't dry out.

beautiful blues

Blue-green foliage is described as glaucous. There are not that many plants that have leaves with a really strong blue cast, but those we have should be treasured for the intense yet tranquil splash of colour they bring to a colour scheme. Hostas are fabulous for retentive soil in shade – *H*. 'Halcyon' and 'Big Daddy' are excellent blue-green varieties. For the sun, try *Hebe* 'Clear Skies' and the rue *Ruta graveolens* 'Jackman's Blue', but plant the rue out of reach as it can cause bad skin irritations to sensitive skin. Several conifers possess outstandingly beautiful blue foliage, notably *Cedrus atlantica* 'Glauca', junipers such as *J. squamata* 'Blue Carpet' and *J.s.* 'Blue Star' and many *Picea pungens* varieties.

Although grey and silver plants are easy to place and work with, take care not to overdo the quantities or the border could easily end up looking dull and lifeless. Remember that the true value of these blue-leaved plants is as mixers with other colours.

leaf and plant size

The hostas just mentioned have strong, eye-catching leaves, but most of the plants with silver-grey foliage contribute a soft, hazy effect to a planting. A couple of notable exceptions are the giant Scotch thistle (*Onopordum nervosum*), which stands as tall as a man and is strongly silver in the sunshine, and *Salvia argentea*, with enormous furry white leaves like those of a giant flop-eared rabbit.

left: *Ruta graveolens* 'Jackman's Blue' looks fabulous, but avoid contact with skin.

below: The silver, woolly leaves of *Stachys byzantina* 'Big Ears' are an effective contrast to many different plants.

star combinations

While these pale colours go well almost anywhere, they are outstanding in certain pairings:

● Glaucous leaves with blue and white flowers, also with purple foliage.

● Silver and grey with pastels such as mauve, pink or apricot

● Bright silver as a glittering contrast to indigo blue or hot pinks and reds

● Silver with purple flowers and leaves, to bring sparkle to sombre shades.

left: *Hosta* 'Halcyon' is one of the most intense blue foliage plants.

left: Reaching for the sky, the jagged silver leaves of *Onopordum* take centre stage.

below: *Ballota pseudodictamnus* forms a spreading mound of felted leaves.

below: With its filigree foliage, *Artemisia* 'Powis Castle' is one of the finest silver plants.

top 10 silver and blue foliage plants

1 *Artemisia* **'Powis Castle'** Always a favourite choice for a silver shrub, this forms a good-sized hummock, and its finely cut leaves are a good, bright silver – some other artemisias are distinctly grey in comparison.

2 *Ballota pseudodictamnus* A pale silver-green little evergreen, softly furry all over its stems and leaves.

3 *Festuca glauca* A neat, tufty grass with a distinctly blue tinge to its blades. The tussocks remain all year and look brilliant after a frosty night, but festuca is at its bluest when its new growth has coloured up in spring.

4 *Helichrysum petiolare* This tender little plant is apt to sprawl, which makes it very popular for summer containers and baskets. Its all-over furry greyness is appealing in the sun but it looks very sad in grey weather.

5 *Hosta* **'Halcyon'** One of the bluest-leaved of all hostas, its ribbed leaves keep their colour best in the shade.

6 *Juniperus horizontalis* **'Glauca'** The smoky blue of blue conifers is a good mixer, and this one makes a low, spreading mat that looks at once solid and cloudy.

7 *Onopordum nervosum* There is no mistaking this spiky, spiny giant thistle. Stem, prickly leaves and flower buds are all covered in white felt, which makes it a real eye-catcher.

8 *Rhamnus alaternus* **'Argenteovariegata'** Buckthorns are useful hardy shrubs, but this one is far more attractive than its workaday cousins. Its grey-green leaves are edged with a broad white margin that gives it much greater style and appeal.

9 *Ruta graveolens* **'Jackman's Blue'** Rue makes a neat mound of sea-blue leaves, each finely cut but with noticeably round ends. A very pretty little herb, and highly aromatic, but not one for the kitchen. The yellow flowers are not much of an attraction.

10 *Santolina pinnata* **subsp.** *neapolitana* A dense mass of wispy stems gives the impression of a rounded silver cloud. Santolinas look good planted en masse and are at their most silvery on poor soil.

right: Neat little 'hedgehogs' of *Festuca glauca* provide excellent all-year colour.

yellows and golds

Yellow and golden leaves bring sunshine to the garden whatever the weather. Their colour is often as brilliant as any flower, but far better because it lasts a great deal longer. Such gleaming foliage is enormously useful to cheer up a gloomy corner, too. However, despite its glowing appeal it is as well to be cautious when using yellow foliage, for the brighter shades are extremely dominant and can easily cause a planting to become unbalanced if used in too great a quantity. An excess of yellow foliage can make a planting look bleached out, artificial and even sickly. The exception to this rule is in a golden border where the effect is very obviously an intended one. But if they are used in moderation, gold and yellow leaves make a truly invaluable contribution to a planting.

shades of yellow and gold

Leaves with gold and green variegations are the easiest to use and most versatile of all the yellow-leaved plants, for the green in the leaf calms down the vitality of the gold, yet still benefits from the gold's brightness. Many hollies and ivies have this colour combination, as do variegated varieties of eleagnus and euonymus and the golden-leaved privet, *Ligustrum ovalifolium* 'Aureum'.

Soft lemons and limes are colourful without being too bold, and are extremely easy to incorporate into almost any planting to give it an overall lift. The shrubby honeysuckle *Lonicera nitida* 'Lemon Beauty' lives up to its name, while low-growing soft yellows include *Lysimachia nummularia* 'Aurea' and the golden grass, *Milium effusum* 'Aureum'.

sunshine yellows

Sunshine yellow is striking and brings colour and excitement to a planting, but should be used with a little caution. The golden-leaved choisyas, *C.* 'Sundance' and the tapering-leaved *C.* 'Goldfingers', make good specimen plants, while the shrubby honeysuckle, *Lonicera nitida* 'Baggesen's Gold', and *Physocarpus opulifolius* 'Dart's Gold', are both a mass of small bright yellow foliage. Golden conifers vary from greeny gold to a truly brassy old-gold; the neatly conical *Thuja occidentalis* 'Rheingold' turns quite red-gold in winter.

Yellows that have a flush of orange can be hard to place, but work incredibly well in the right company. Trees such as *Robinia pseudoacacia* 'Frisia' and the golden elder, *Sambucus racemosa* 'Plumosa Aurea' look marvellous against a dark green or blue-green background. Even more orange is a truly brassy shrub, *Spiraea japonica* 'Goldflame'. Rich blues look terrific with it, and so do orange flowers.

left: Grow *Coprosma* 'Gold Splash' in a sheltered spot.

right: Easy and quick-growing, golden privet (*Ligustrum ovalifolium* 'Aureum') creates a splash of colour almost anywhere.

below: The leaves of *Jasminum officinale* add a final burst of colour to this pretty plant.

Certain yellow-leaved plants can be scorched by hot midday sun. These include *Acer shirasawanum* f. *aureum*, *Aucuba japonica* 'Crotonifolia', *Berberis thunbergii* 'Aurea', *Philadelphus coronarius* 'Aureus' and some of the hostas. Site them carefully so they are out of the brightest midday rays, but with plenty of sun at other times as the leaves do not develop their brightest golden colouring if they are given too much shade.

leaf and plant size

Apart from the shade of yellow, the size of the individual leaves and the plant itself has a great influence on the amount of impact it creates. Large-leaved plants seek attention, and adding a bright leaf colour will further intensify this effect, so large-leaved yellow plants such as choisya and elder (*Sambucus*) need to be placed with even greater care. By contrast, small-leaved plants and slender ones such as grasses blend in much more readily and are immensely useful for creating some extra brightness without being overwhelming.

star combinations

To make the most of the power of yellow, try some of the following:

● Brassy gold with intense blue flowers

● Soft yellow with lime-green flowers for a subtle harmony.

● Greenish or pale yellow with purple foliage: a striking contrast to be used in moderation

● Sunny yellow with yellow and orange flowers for an uplifting harmony

● Gold with white and cream flowers for a soft and refreshing mix

left: The golden cut-leaved elder (*Sambucus racemosa* 'Plumosa Aurea') has shoots that are bronze-yellow when young.

below: Glossy evergreen leaves of *Elaeagnus* x *ebbingei* 'Gilt Edge'.

top 10 yellow foliage plants

1 *Elaeagnus x ebbingei* **'Gilt Edge'** A deservedly popular choice for a golden-variegated shrub, you can rely on its dense clothing of green and gold leaves to provide a welcome splash of colour all year round.

2 *Euonymus japonicus* **'Ovatus Aureus'** The broad yellow band around its glossy leaves gives this euonymus a bright look. The balance of green and gold allows it link other greens and golds in a planting and its solid, dense shape, especially if kept trimmed, make it an effective companion to more feathery evergolds, such as conifers.

3 *Gleditsia triacanthos* **'Sunburst'** A tree that lives up to its name, as its new foliage bursts out, sunshine yellow, in the spring. The ferny leaves get greener through the summer and then brilliant gold before falling in the autumn.

4 *Hakonechloa macra* **'Aureola'** A low, arching grass with broad blades of gold thinly striped with green. It's an easy mixer and wonderfully effective at lightening a planting that looks a little heavy or dark.

5 *Humulus lupulus* **'Aureus'** Each year the golden hop grows from nothing into a tangle of twining stems that can cover a large arch or arbour. It is lime green in shade and pale gold in sunshine, and will often be an attractive mixture of the two as it grows up into the light. The hops that appear in late summer are also pale gold.

6 *Ilex x altaclarensis* **'Golden King'** Among the several variegated hollies, 'Golden King' is an excellent variety. As it is not particularly noted for its berries, it is an especially good choice for hedging, as regular trimming will ensure there is plenty of new growth, which is more brightly gold-rimmed than old leaves.

7 *Lysimachia nummularia* **'Aurea'** This is creeping Jenny, and its long stems do indeed creep enthusiastically, rooting as they go, to form a butter yellow mat from spring to autumn, enhanced by golden flowers.

8 *Pleioblastus auricomus* A bamboo with its focus of interest in the long leaves rather than the canes. These stick out horizontally all the way up the stems, their bold green and yellow stripes even showier in strong sunshine.

9 *Sambucus racemosa* **'Plumosa Aurea'** This is often recommended as a faster-growing, less fussy alternative to a golden-leaved maple. Its lacy leaves, which open auburn and fade to a golden glow, are its great attraction, and it is happy to be pruned to encourage more new golden growth.

10 *Vinca minor* **'Illumination'** Periwinkles are enthusiastic groundcoverers and 'Illumination' soon creates a golden pool or cascade of trailing stems clothed in small pointed leaves broadly splashed with lemon yellow. The deep blue flowers are a lovely contrast.

right: *Hakonechloa macra* 'Aureola' forms a fountain of gold leaves.

reds, purples and bronzes

Dark-coloured foliage adds a remarkable degree of depth and contrast to a planting. The rich shades of purple and red are supremely dramatic, glowing like sullen jewels against a backcloth of paler colours. However, caution is the watchword here, as lots of dark foliage can create a very sombre, gloomy atmosphere. Used sparingly and with plenty of other, lighter colours to give plenty of sparkle, these rich foliage shades can add immeasurably to the whole look of a planting, creating wonderful effects of depth and colour. Lighter shades of red and purple, and earthy browns and bronzes, can be used more freely to create subtle accents within a planting.

shades of purples

The deepest purples and dark reds look hugely dramatic and immediately leap out visually, especially on large-leaved plants. Shrubs with smaller leaves, such as *Acer palmatum* varieties, smoke bushes (*Cotinus coggygria*) and purple-leaved elder (*Sambucus*) varieties, do not demand attention quite so insistently and are easier to place in the garden. The same goes for small plants like heucheras.

Lighter reds and purples that are suffused with a softer shade or only apply to young growth that later turns green are much more amenable and easy to use in the garden. Less attention-seeking than the darkest shades, they still stand out from their more mundane neighbours. The little *Saxifraga fortunei* has red undersides to their leaves, while the purple-flushed variety of the bean tree, *Catalpa* x *erubescens* 'Purpurea', turns from rich purple to green as the foliage matures. Purple fennel (*Foeniculum vulgare* 'Purpureum') and *Pennisetum setaceum* 'Rubrum' a feathery grass, are both infinitely light and cloudy, and *Chamaecyparis thyoides* 'Ericoides' is a fluffy-looking conifer with a reddish cast at some times of the year.

Avoid massive plants with solid dark purple foliage, for they are just too dark and soak up all the light. Examples are the tree *Acer platanoides* 'Crimson King' and the large shrub or small tree *Corylus maxima* 'Purpurea'. Also, avoid an excess of purple in a part of the garden that will be used in the evening as it will create a gloomy atmosphere.

earth colours

Earthy browns and bronzes are too often overlooked as 'non-colours' or ignored for their subtlety, but look immensely appealing

left: Many plants, such as *Parthenocissus tricuspidata*, develop spectacular leaf colour in autumn.

right: The glowing red stems of ruby chard (*Beta vulgaris*) make this vegetable worthy of a prime position.

below: The large leaves of *Catalpa erubescens* 'Purpurea' are purple when young.

against the right background. Most striking are the ornamental grasses *Carex buchananii* and *Uncinia uncinata rubra*, which look good all year but come into their own in winter against a background of contrasting foliage.

leaf and plant size

Purple and reds that combine with an architectural shape or bold leaves are the real prima donnas of the garden, and need to be kept close to the house or used as 'punctuation marks' at definite sites within a planting. These include spiky-leaved phormiums and cordylines, of which there is a number of dark varieties, *Begonia* 'Dragon Wing' and the large, long-fingered leaves and purple stems of the imposing *Ricinus communis* 'Impala'.

star combinations

Using purple, red and bronze foliage is a chance for some really dramatic plantings.

● Rich purple foliage with flowers in a similar but slightly lighter shade, lightened by pink flowers and silver foliage

● Dark purple with clear red flowers

● Rich purple together with white flowers and fresh green foliage

● Bright red or red-flushed foliage with dark blue flowers and grey or silver foliage.

● Red foliage with lime-green.

● Bronze foliage with yellow flowers

left: A fireworks display of autumn colour from *Acer japonicum* 'Vitifolium'.

right: The bronzed, feathery foliage of *Foeniculum vulgare* 'Purpureum' creates lovely see-through effects.

top 10 purple, red and bronze foliage plants

1 *Acer japonicum* **'Vitifolium'** An elegant, bush, large shrub or small tree; the mid-green lobed leaves look like they have been set on fire in autumn when the whole plant turns bright red.

2 *Begonia* **'Dragon Wing'** Gorgeously coloured like crushed velvet, this is one that will need to come indoors for the winter, but in summer its richness will make a wonderful centrepiece for an exotic container planting.

3 *Beta vulgaris* **'Ruby Chard'** A vegetable that looks too good for the vegetable patch, it is often used decoratively – although picking the young leaves to eat will encourage yet more growth. The broad stems are a glowing scarlet that spreads along the veins of the dark green leaves, giving an overall flushed appearance from a distance.

4 *Cotinus* **'Grace'** The smoke bush gets its name from the little puffs of cloudy flowers it sends up in late summer, but the whole shrub has a slightly smoky look to it, each insubstantial round leaf flushed red and purple.

5 *Euphorbia dulcis* **'Chameleon'** Not a euphorbia that grows too tall, but it will provide a forest of purple-tinted stems clothed in richly coloured leaves that colour even more brilliantly in the autumn.

6 *Foeniculum vulgare* **'Purpureum'** This is called bronze fennel, but the tall stems and feathery plumes are subtly flushed with greens, creams, purple and mauve. The overall effect is of a smoky cloud that looks wonderful against a contrasting solid background or mingling with large flowers such as roses. Its subtle colouring blends with almost any other colour.

7 *Heuchera* Several varieties of these easy-going perennials have purple leaves; others, with a slight purple cast to the upper side of the leaf, give a hint of the deep scarlet undersides.

8 *Phormium* Phormiums form a large fountain of arching blades, giving them the appearance of a cross between an exotic grass and a half-buried palm tree. There are many varieties in shades of bronze, red and purple, many of them striped along the length of the leaves, and new ones are appearing all the time.

9 *Physocarpus opulifolius* **'Diabolo'** An all-over dark purple that could be too sombre on a heavier-looking shrub, but this has just enough lightness – airy without looking sparse – to prove a good but unimposing contrast in a mixed planting.

10 *Sambucus nigra* **'Black Beauty'** Each narrow leaflet of the purple elder's large leaves looks as if it has been stained by the juice of its own berries, and in late summer the berries themselves hang in abundant purple-black trusses. A most attractive shrub that will soon grown into a small tree unless kept trimmed.

variegations

A plant that is described as variegated combines two or more colours in its leaves. Green leaves with a margin or central splash of white, cream or yellow occur most widely and such plants look delightful – the touch of pale colour is like the sparkle of sunshine on water, bringing the garden to life. While green variegations are the easiest ones to incorporate into a scheme, there are less usual ones that look outstanding in the right company. The purple or brown-marked green leaves of *Tiarella* 'Mint Chocolate' and *Geranium phaeum* 'Samobor', for example, look fantastic when grown alongside plants with purple leaves, while the golden variegated foliage of such striking plants as *Elaeagnus* x *ebbingei* 'Gilt Edge' and *Euonymus fortunei* 'Emerald 'n' Gold' makes a glorious combination with yellow-flowered plants.

varieties of variegation

Variegation comes in many forms other than contrasting margins and central markings. The geranium just mentioned, for example, has a distinctive brown horseshoe shape on its rounded leaves. Sometimes central splashes are so large the effect is more like a cream or yellow leaf with a green margin; these are particularly vulnerable to scorching. Stripes also occur frequently, especially on long leaves such as grasses, phormiums and bamboos. There are spotted and marbled leaves, too, and some patterns that are so mottled or blotched the plant looks diseased. Not all variegation is limited to two colours: *Hydrangea macrophylla* 'Quadricolor' has leaves that are divided into four distinct shades of green, and *Actinidia kolomikta*, which is related to the kiwi vine, has heart shaped leaves in bold bands of green, white and pink.

Used in moderation, variegated foliage adds greatly to colour in the garden. Cream or white variegated leaves really pep up a planting and are great for enlivening gloomy spots. In order to be seen at their best, such plants need to be seen against a contrasting background such as mid to dark green or purple foliage, a dark fence or a wall. Pairing variegated foliage with flowers that pick up on the secondary colour – yellow narcissi with *Euonymus fortunei* 'Emerald 'n' Gold', *Fuchsia magellanica* 'Versicolor' at the base of a pinkish mauve clematis, for example – can work extremely effectively, but avoid placing variegated plants next to each other or they will fight each other and detract from the impact you intend.

right: The marbled leaves of Arum *italicum* 'Marmoratum' make good winter groundcover.

below: Neat white edging outlines the spines on *Ilex aquifolium* 'Silver King'.

below right: The striped foliage of *Sisyrinchium striatum* 'Aunt May' makes the vertical leaves more prominent.

left: *Euonymus fortunei* 'Silver Queen' is a versatile grower with evergreen foliage.

above: A tough and tolerant shrub, *Cornus alba* 'Elegantissima' is also good for winter interest.

right: *Iris pallida* 'Variegata' has the bonus of pale blue flowers.

top 10 variegated foliage plants

1 *Arum italicum* **'Marmoratum'** These are wonderful for winter interest with attractive foliage from early winter through into spring. The leaves are large, arrow-shaped, and beautifully marbled with pale green and cream.

2 *Cornus alba* **'Elegantissima'** An easy and fast-growing, variegated dogwood with green and white leaves from spring to autumn. These fall to reveal bright red stems for winter colour.

3 *Cornus controversa* **'Variegata'** The wedding cake tree is well named. Its tiers of branches are clothed with leaves that have broad white edges, and the whole effect is enhanced in summer when the leaves are topped with white flowers.

4 *Euonymus fortunei* **'Silver Queen'** This easy, evergreen shrub looks good all year with its shiny, oval, white-edged green leaves. It grows equally well as groundcover or clambering slowly up a wall or fence.

5 *Euphorbia cjaracoas* **'Silver Swan'** This spurge forms a handsome clump of upright stems clothed with long, tapered, grey-green leaves that are widely edged with creamy-white.

6 *Hosta* These lush, large-leaved perennials are invaluable for foliage interest in shady spots, and variegated varieties such as 'Thomas Hogg' are excellent for brightening a gloomy spot.

7 *Ilex aquifolium* These hollies are superb structural plants that eventually reach small-tree size. Those with variegated foliage show up beautifully against a dark background. These include 'Argentea Marginata', 'Ferox Argentea' and 'Silver Queen'.

8 *Iris pallida* **'Variegata'** The spiky, grey-green and white-striped leaves are lightly flushed with yellow, and make an immensely effective contrast to many other border plants, with the bonus of large pale blue flowers, too.

9 *Sisyrinchium striatum* **'Aunt May'** This good border plant forms clumps of spiky, iris-like foliage edged with cream and pale yellow, and bears stems of many small, creamy-yellow flowers in summer.

10 *Vinca minor* **'Argenteovariegata'** The cream-edged evergreen leaves of this lesser periwinkle make excellent groundcover in almost all situations, and show up its deep blue flowers to perfection.

using colour

colour and light

The aspect of a planting site – that is, the amount of sun or shade it receives – has a great influence on the plants you choose. While a few plants are go-anywhere creatures that thrive in both sun and shade, most have a distinct preference for one or the other. Luckily, plants tend to look best in a situation that suits them.

right: Soft colours for shade are provided by lush, large-leaved hostas and tree ferns.

sunlight and shade

The sun's rays enhance the vitality of colourful plants and bring their full beauty to life. Most plants thrive in sun so there is certainly plenty of choice, but it's important to differentiate between sun for only part of the day and a complete lack of shade. To stand out in all-day bright sunlight, colours need to be bright and bold – deep blue, rich orange, bright red and dark purple – and with more emphasis on coloured foliage; variegated leaves can look washed-out. Where a site only receives sun for part of the day the colours that look best are altogether softer, such as richer shades of pastels like mid-blue and yellow, pink and mauve, offset by silver or variegated leaves.

Shade, so often perceived as 'difficult', is easy to plant from a colour point of view. Few rich-hued plants thrive in shade, but sunless sites cry out for lots of pale flowers and foliage to lighten the gloom. Foliage variegated with silver and gold is invaluable for cheering up a dark, gloomy spot and will prefer shelter from too much scorching sun. Many shade-loving plants also have glossy leaves that will help reflect the light.

moving shadows

Take time to become familiar with how sun and shade fall in your garden. Every season will be different as not only the height of the sun but the shade from trees will alter from month to month. If you have just taken on a new garden, you will really need to experience a whole year's cycle of the seasons. Make notes on a regular basis, because it is surprisingly difficult to recall, on a hot summer's day, just how much or little light reaches your plot in the depths of winter.

above: Most brightly coloured plants prefer to be planted in full sun, where their vivid shades sparkle with life.

top 10 plants for shade

A good selection of shrubs and smaller plants to give year-round structure and interest; perennials for infilling; and flowers for seasonal bursts of soft colour.

1 *Arum italicum* 'Marmoratum'

2 *Dryopteris filix-mas*

3 *Euonymus fortunei* varieties

4 *Fatsia japonica*

5 *Geranium phaeum*

6 *Helleborus orientalis*

7 *Iris foetidissima*

8 *Pulmonaria*

9 *Sarcococca*

10 *Vinca minor* (variegated varieties)

the changing seasons

Light has a **dramatic** effect on the colour and character of plants, yet it is so easy to overlook the changes that take place through the course of a day and from one season to another. The **changing** light **enhances** different colours, so it makes sense to identify how the quality of light alters in your garden, as well as when you will be at home to **appreciate** it.

tip . . .
See for yourself how plants are transformed by the change in light by visiting a nearby garden or park at several different times of day, from very early in the morning to the evening. Visit the same place at different times of year, too, in order to appreciate the changing qualities of light from one season to another. Make a note of the plants you like best.

right: The shapes and colours of alliums and verbascums are enhanced when backlit by the low rays of the sun.

right: Plants with attractive shapes such as *Helleborus argutifolius* look beautiful in winter.

spring

Some plants are nudged back into growth by a rise in temperature, but others are triggered by light levels. This means that, after the all-too-short winter days you can rely on fresh green growth even if there is little warmth. As the season progresses and light levels rise, growth seems unstoppable: the greens will never seem quite so fresh and clean as in spring's clear light, the sight of blossom against a rain-washed sky makes you catch your breath, and Wordsworth's 'host of golden daffodils' shine out even under leaden clouds.

summer and autumn

Take full advantage of slanting light early and late in the day to create some truly magical effects. The low, clear light of early morning is sharp and transparent, while the rays of the evening sun often cast a warm, relaxing haze. At both times of day, pale flowers are brought vividly to life while dark shades such as red and purple appear flat and almost lifeless. Tall, feathery stems, and the flowers and seed-heads of grasses shimmer with hundreds of beads of moisture, and are at their most dramatic when backlit by the sun's rays. Once the sun has set and the light begins to fade the white flowers will take centre stage, appearing to hold on to every last bit of the light and remaining visible long after all of the other colours have faded away into the gathering darkness.

In the middle of the day, when the sun is high, the light can be bright and hard. Now only vivid colours and bold architectural shapes are strong enough to compete with the blazing midday light; pale flowers and airy foliage recede into insignificance.

winter

While the beauty of the winter garden is austere, it can lift the spirits like nothing else at this time of year. The sun is often in short supply, which is all the more reason for making the very most of what light there is. Low winter sunlight picks up every outline of dark evergreens, while yellow evergreens and plants with coloured stems will shine as though lit from within when touched by the sun, and scarce winter flowers sparkle like treasure.

busy lives

You may know the times of day when the sun falls on your garden, but are you going to be there to enjoy it? If you are out at work during the day, identify which parts of your garden get any morning or evening sun. Use the chart below to help choose plants that will enhance your garden, or a particular part of it, for each time of day and year, to bring your garden in tune with the march of the sun and seasons.

Seasonal planting

Summer

morning/evening sun
- plants with soft-coloured flowers
  - white
  - pale yellow
  - soft blue
  - pink
- ornamental grasses
  - *Deschampsia*
  - *Miscanthus sinensis* varieties
  - *Stipa gigantea*
- tall, feathery plants:
  - *Foeniculum vulgare* 'Purpureum'
  - *Verbena bonariensis*

all-day sun
- plants with bold-coloured flowers
  - bright yellow
  - deep blue
  - red
  - orange
  - bright pink
  - purple
- plants with strong, architectural shapes
  - *Cordyline australis*
  - *Cynara cardunculus*
  - *Echinops ritro*
  - phormiums and yuccas

Winter

- yellow evergreens
  - *Elaeagnus* x *ebbingei* 'Gilt Edge'
  - *Choisya ternata* 'Sundance'
- plants with coloured stems
  - *Cornus alba* varieties
  - *Rubus thibetanus*
- Evergreens with structural outlines
  - conifers
  - clipped plants
  - topiaried plants

coping with extremes

While most garden soils are suitable for a wide range of plants, extreme conditions of wet or dry, acid or alkaline soil do occur, and they limit the range of plants that can be grown. While such conditions may seem to be a nuisance at first, they can turn out to be a real asset. Often, conditions can be improved – bulky organic matter is a boon, it will add body to thin, dry soils and, miraculously, also break up heavy clay. The way to easy and rewarding gardening, however, lies in choosing plants that like the conditions on offer rather than to trying to coax along plants that will never feel at home. And plants which enjoy the same conditions automatically tend to look good together and create their own harmonious schemes.

Being guided by colour can help here. Instead of thinking 'I want a pink rose here' and then being disappointed when your rose fails to thrive in the poor, stony soil, think 'I want a bush with large pink summer flowers'. A little research will probably lead you to a pink cistus or sun rose, for which the conditions would be ideal.

left: Moisture-loving iris and *Trollius* thrive in soil that is damp all year.

hostas, ligularias, rheums and gunneras that need a regular supply of water to keep their over-sized leaves in peak condition. A very satisfying picture can be made with all these greens of different hues, shapes and textures, but there is the opportunity for some wonderful colour contrasts too.

Mix in some feathery cream plumes of *Aruncus dioicus* and astilbes (which also come in pink and red), shining yellow kingcups (*Caltha palustris*), and the sunset shades, from pale lemon to deep crimson, of bog primulas such as *Primula. beesiana*, *P. florindae*, *P. pulverulenta* and *P. sikkimensis*. Further colour interest could come from moisture-loving shrubs: the dogwoods (*Cornus alba*) include varieties with white-variegated foliage and gleaming coloured winter stems, while shrubby willows (*Salix*) put on a welcome show of catkins each spring.

avoid ending up with a screaming riot of colour that will not be comfortable to look at or live with. Luckily there is a fair choice of varieties in softer shades too, making it possible to concentrate on one main colour – such as red – and harmonize it with paler shades and bicolors along with plenty of white and cream to act as a buffer.

All of these gorgeous shrubs flower in the main from late winter to early summer, and a common problem, therefore, is that the later seasons can seem flat in comparison, with heavy evergreen leaves dominating for the rest of the year. For a succession of colour, ftry adding some later-flowering shrubs such as hydrangeas and *Kalmia latifolia*, perennials such as *Kirengeshoma* for flowers and hostas for foliage, as well as evergreens such as pernettyas and skimmias that both have showy autumn berries.

colour in a dry garden

Among the range of strategies for survival that drought-tolerant plants have evolved, a common one is silver or grey foliage. Many, such as artemisias, lavenders and stachys (appropriately called lamb's ears) are finely dissected or covered in hairs to give a soft, fuzzy look. These are all good choices, but don't overdo it or the garden could look ashen and lifeless on overcast days. Perk up the colour range with acid-green *Santolina rosmarinifolia*, golden thymes and purple sedums. Greys and silvers also make a marvellous foil to vivid flower colours that can bring the garden to shimmering, vibrant life, like deep blue ceanothus, pink and purple cistus, yellow brooms (*Cytisus*) and purple *Verbena bonariensis*.

in the wet

Where soil is permanently and naturally moist there is a fantastic opportunity to go for the lush, leafy approach and grow some of those magnificent, large-leaved perennials such as

the acid touch

Certain plants must grow on acid soil and will sicken and die if grown on soil that is contains lime, which is referred to as alkaline soil. If you garden on acid soil, you have the luck to be able to grow some real beauties which cannot be grown successfully on alkaline soil. There is no lack of colourful impact from camellias, pieris and rhododendrons (including azaleas) – indeed, a little careful selection is necessary to

tip . . .

If you yearn for these colourful spring beauties but your soil is alkaline, you can still grow the more compact varieties in large containers or raised beds filled with lime-free (ericaceous) potting compost or imported acid topsoil. Don't bother attempting to grow them in a border with added peat, as the lime will soon infiltrate the acid peat and the plants' roots will make their way into the surrounding alkaline soil.

below: Rhododendrons need acid soil, but compact ones such as *R. yakushimanum* can be grown in containers.

creating illusions with colour

One of the most **fascinating** properties of colour is that it can actually be used to fool the eye and create **illusions** of scale and distance. Crafty **placing** of colours can make all the difference to how your garden appears, however large or small it may be in reality.

right: Soft coloured plants such as these blue delphiniums appear to recede, while white flowers catch the eye.

manipulating space

Bright colours immediately catch the eye and appear to leap forward, while cool colours recede, appearing further away than in reality. You can create a feeling of distance in a limited space simply by gathering all the bright, attention-seeking colours near the house and placing the pale ones further away. Most effective of all is to plant the furthest part of the garden with foliage in muted shades such as blue-green or green tinged with purple, creating the impression of a misty, subtle vista that disappears into the distance. The same principle can be adopted by using coloured paints or wood stains to transform background walls or fences. Where a solid boundary is not essential, replace it with a fence of an open design to create a feeling of space and airiness.

While colour plays the most important role in creating illusions, plant and flower shape is important too. Large-leaved architectural plants are naturally dramatic in appearance and so draw attention to themselves, even at a distance. The huge leaves of acanthus and *Rheum* (ornamental rhubarb) have this quality, as do the sword-shaped leaves of plants such as cordylines, phormiums and yuccas. As with bright colours, these plants should be placed near the house rather than in the distance where they would foreshorten the view. The same goes for flower size. Misty masses of the tiny white blooms of *Crambe cordifolia* and *Gypsophila paniculata* are ideal for distance planting, whereas large blooms like peonies and many bright-coloured roses are too attention-seeking in that role.

This principle can be effective in creating a feeling of depth in individual borders as well as the entire garden, by placing softer colours at the back and the brighter ones and bold shapes towards the front. Even if the whole border is planted to a brightly coloured scheme, the impact will be greater if vibrant flowers and foliage are leavened with some softer shades or with foliage. Too much of a strong colour or mix of colours can appear to be over-emphatic and destroy the feeling of depth that you want.

a whiter shade of pale

Although white is a cool colour, bright white flowers actually seize the eye in a similar way to bright colours. For distance planting the answer is to use creamy-white blooms which are much more mellow and soft in appearance. White is particularly pleasing near the house and around the patio, as it catches every last scrap of evening light and looks almost luminous in the twilight. As a backdrop to planting, either as a fence or wall, bright white also has its drawbacks. The contrast that it makes with bold colours can be uncomfortably raw and stark, and it will too often appear grey in dull weather and when pale creams and yellows are set against it. Cream often works better.

above: Brilliantly coloured tulips appear almost to 'float' above a carpet of beautiful blue forget-me-nots (*Myosotis*).

colourful illusions

cool, receding colours and shapes

- soft pastel shades like pink, yellow, blue and cream

- silver foliage

- blue-green and purple-tinged leaves

- a profusion of tiny flowers

warm, advancing colours and shapes

- yellow or gold-variegated foliage

- bright green leaves

- flowers in bright yellow, red, orange and purple

- large, stark white flowers

- deep purple foliage

- plants with large leaves

- architectural plants that have a bold shape

small gardens

The trend these days to ever-smaller gardens calls for a **canny** approach to get the very best from a limited space. While keen gardeners are always tempted to try a little of everything, the result can easily be messy, with lots of different colours fussing and arguing with each other, creating a **busy** atmosphere that is never entirely enjoyable. In a small space the key to success is to keep things **simple**, for too much cluttered colour will make the plot appear even smaller than it actually is.

right: Keep colour schemes simple using an abundance of green and softly coloured foliage.

right: Structural evergreens such as these clipped box shapes (*Buxus*) are great for year-round interest.

year-round interest

Small gardens tend to be on view all the time, so presenting a pleasing scene right through the year is of prime importance. The best way to achieve this is by first choosing structural plants to form the 'backbone' of the garden and then adding other plants to create a succession of colour through each season. So, for example, the year could start with spring bulbs, closely followed by herbaceous perennials along with flowering shrubs for every season, plus annuals and tender perennials to fill any gaps from summer to autumn, all of them held together with carefully selected evergreens and other plants that will look good all year.

Pay particular attention when choosing the largest plants, for in small gardens these must really pull their weight and be attractive for as long as possible. One-season wonders have no place here – seasonal performers must have at least two periods of interest, such as spring flowers and autumn fruit, or they need to have long-lasting attributes like attractive

foliage. It is tempting to choose evergreens, and these are indeed invaluable, but too many can create a static, dull, atmosphere (a useful rule of thumb is to keep the proportion of all medium to large plants about one-third evergreen, two-thirds deciduous). See the Planting chapter (pages 116–129) for some helpful suggestions. Planting in layers (see page 121) is an invaluable technique in a small garden.

Play it safe and classic with schemes that are composed of pale colours, because this will help to create the illusion of greater space. Such a colour scheme will also promote an atmosphere of calm, peace and harmony. Relating colours inside the house to those immediately outside, will make indoors appear to slip seamlessly into the outdoors, giving a greater feeling of unity and space.

The adventurous alternative is to go completely the other way and create a dramatic, theatrical look by turning over the whole garden to striking foliage plants and bright colours.

left: Garden upwards using tall plants such as angelica, and tripods for climbers.

going up

If you cannot garden outwards, garden upwards. While ground space may be restricted, vertical space certainly is not. Boundary walls and fences are not only ideal as ready-made sites for climbers and wall shrubs, but clothing the boundaries in plants also makes the garden seem larger by disguising where your plot ends and the one next door begins.

Vertical features can be incorporated into even the smallest garden, introducing a whole new dimension and creating more planting space as well. A pergola is a superb feature to create dappled shade over a sunny patio, an arbour can be tucked into a corner, while arches fit easily over paths and gateways. Obelisks or pyramids can be dropped into borders or containers for instant height.

The treatment of boundary walls, fences and screens is particularly important in a small space, for with a little forethought your boundaries can appear to recede rather than advance. Paint walls and fences with light-coloured, but not bright, paint or wood stain such as cream (preferable to white), sage green or pale sea blue.

larger gardens

More space gives more **freedom** to the range of colours and plants, but colour planning is even more essential without the discipline of choice imposed by the restriction of a small garden.

The principle of brighter colours near the house, receding colours at the boundaries is equally valid in a larger plot. Think also about concentrating winter colour near the house, where you can **appreciate** it from indoors. Quiet, receding colours and fuzzy shapes will increase the sense of distance to a long view, and you also have the chance to visually 'borrow' from neighbouring gardens or open country if your own boundaries are only subtly delineated.

If the whole area is open, think about creating some divisions using borders, hedges or screens. Preventing the entire garden from being visible all at once will introduce an element of **surprise** and allow you to create areas that have a distinctly different feel. A garden-within-a-garden could be as boldly coloured and theatrical as you like without having a jarring effect on the garden at large, and an enclosed one-colour border would not be spoilt by intruding colours from nearby.

colour through the year

early spring

The **rebirth** of the garden with its **exuberant** burst of regeneration and new life never fails to **quicken** the pulse after the gloom of winter. Days that are lengthening and **warmer** temperatures bring about a veritable **explosion** of plant growth, making the face of the garden change **dramatically** from week to week. All the colours of the season work well together, though be wary of putting too much pink and yellow together.

below: Blue *Pulmonaria* is superb for underplanting shrubs and trees.

above: *Primula vulgaris* (primrose) is an enchanting soft yellow.

yellow

Yellow gives a welcoming feel to the start of the year, and ranges from palest lemon to vibrant gold.

Shrubs are the stalwarts of the yellows, with some handsome winter-flowerers continuing to perform into the spring. Favourites include fragrant mahonias with their spiky evergreen leaves, and the gorgeous witch-hazels (*Hamamelis*) with the spicily scented little knots of flowers. These hardy performers are joined by forsythia which, although a ubiquitous plant of the season, is worth having if space permits. Choose between large and lurid yellow flowers of *Forsythia* x *intermedia* 'Lynwood' and 'Spring Glory' or the softer yellow of *F. suspensa*.

Early bulbs – crocuses, early narcissi and daffodils – burst upon the scene and look their most glorious when planted in golden pools and drifts. Yet the most enchanting yellow of the season belongs to that shy and delicate woodlander, the primrose (*Primula vulgaris*), which looks delightful when massed together in shady spots.

blue

Many spring flowers are a deep, clear blue, like fragments of clear sky fallen to earth

Bulbs, perennials and clematis offer some exceptionally beautiful shades of blue. Drifts of dainty little bulbs such as glory-of-the-snow (*Chionodoxa*) and *Scilla sibirica* look marvellous in borders, as do clumps of *Pulmonaria* (lungwort) – *P. angustifolia* 'Mawson's Blue' is one with flowers of the deepest colour. On walls, fences, obelisks and even other, well-established plants, the well-behaved *Clematis alpina* and *C. macropetala* species offer pretty hanging bells in almost every shade of blue, from the pale lavender of the fluffy double 'Maidwell Hall' to the dark, almost royal blue of 'Pamela Jackman'. Both leaves and blooms of these clematis look so ethereal and delicate that it seems impossible that they can survive so early in the year, but in fact they are tough and easy to grow.

pink

Pink adds a touch of sweetness to a planting Winter performers like *Viburnum bodnantense* and winter cherry (*Prunus subhirtella*) are encouraged by the kinder weather to produce a final show of beautiful blooms in the palest of shell pink. Beneath, echo the colour with carpets of winter-flowering heathers (*Erica carnea*) that have flowers in many shades of pink, as do many of the *Helleborus orientalis* (Lenten rose). Bergenias, aptly called elephant's ears, not only have dense flowerheads in a variety of pinks, but their tough and leathery leaves are often flushed with dark pink and red, with deeply coloured

above: *Bergenia* has useful evergreen foliage as well as pretty pink flowerheads.

above: The flowers of *Leucojum aestivum* are more aristocratic versions of those of the snowdrops (*Galanthus*).

undersides. Walls and fences can be brought to life with flowering quinces like *Chaenomeles* x *superba* 'Pink Lady', which bears blooms along its naked branches. If you are attracted to the bright sugar-pinks of some flowering cherries, they will need careful placing, and avoid them in close proximity to the strong yellows of daffodils and forsythia.

Pinks predominate among camellias, though other shades such as white and red are widely available. Camellias usually need the shelter of a wall, too, in order to protect their huge and luscious flowers, though avoid early morning sun as this can damage frosted blooms. And while the pinkish-white flowers of *Daphne odora* 'Aureomarginata' are nowhere near as showy, their fragrance is second to none.

white

White brings unsullied freshness to the garden, its associations of innocence and purity a lovely introduction to the growing season.

Most of the spring-flowering whites are easy-to-grow, tolerant plants. The evergreen winter-flowering *Viburnum tinus* carries on well into spring, to be joined by *Spiraea thunbergii*, and, if the weather is kind, *Magnolia stellata*. Down at ground level you can have drifts of white winter-flowering heathers with that harbinger of spring, the snowdrop, followed by pools of white crocuses.

how to create spring harmonies

As the colour range of early spring is limited, turn this to your advantage by using just one colour in an area of the garden. Employ a whole range of shades within that one colour – with yellow, for example, there is plenty of choice, from palest primrose through lemon-yellow and glowing gold. Unfurling foliage provides a rich complement, particularly with yellow-greens such as the new leaves of *Valeriana phu* 'Aurea' and the golden grass blades of *Milium effusum* 'Aureum'.

In the scramble for brightness after the dark of winter it is easy to fall into the trap of massing lots of different colours and creating some really discordant combinations. This is particularly easy to do with spring bulbs, as when planting in autumn it's very hard to imagine those dry bulbs as substantial and colourful plants. Try planting bulbs in plain plastic pots and then, when they are close to flowering, sink potfuls of them into just the right positions.

late spring

As the soil absorbs the warmth of the sun and showers of rain, the tempo of growth quickens significantly. With plants bursting into flower on every day that passes, the range of colours really begins to expand, and some bold, bright hues make an entrance. Brightest of all are bulbs – wonderful for creating an additional layer of interest and for cheering up those parts of the garden that become dark and gloomy later on. Amid all this beauty the contribution of one colour is often overlooked: green. Never more glorious than in this season, with the freshly unfurled leaves as yet untouched by the ravages of weather and pests. Spring greens make the perfect backdrop to every colour at this time of year.

above: The brilliantly coloured blooms of *Tulipa* 'Couleur Cardinal' show up against its leaves.

red

Red brings a feeling of warmth that is in tune with the lengthening days and heralds the forthcoming riches of summer

Tulips are the only spring bulb in red, but what reds there are. Choose from among the short-stemmed Greggii varieties that have the added bonus of patterned leaves, or tall-stemmed ones like *Tulipa praestens* 'Fusilier', the classically shaped 'Apeldoorn' or the wine-dark peony-flowered 'Uncle Tom'.

If your garden is on acid soil, there is a host of glorious red blooms on offer, from azaleas, camellias, crinodendron and rhododendrons, plus the flame-red young growths of pieris. On unsuitable, alkaline, soils, you could try growing compact varieties of these spring beauties in containers filled with ericaceous (lime-free) compost.

yellow

Yellow becomes more brazen and dominant, with rich bronze-yellow as well as clear sunshine golds.

Bulbs that start off this season are the later-flowering narcissi, followed by a whole range of tulips. Formal in appearance, tulips are fabulous for seasonal planting schemes along with spring bedding plants. Perennials such as fluffy-flowered rock-dweller *Aurinia saxitalis*, the cheerful dandelion-like *Doronicum* and cowslips (*Primula veris*) carry the colour into more informal areas. In ponds and bog gardens, bright yellow is predominant too, with kingcups or marsh marigold (*Caltha palustris*), water buttercups (*Ranunculus lingua* 'Grandiflorus') and globe flowers (*Trollius* x *cultorum*), as well as the showy spathes of *Lysichiton americanus* (skunk cabbage), rising like canary-coloured daggers from the water.

Softer creamy yellows at this time of the year include the lovely *Clematis montana* 'Primrose Star', which is much more compact and less thuggish that most other montanas, and Warminster broom (*Cytisus* x *praecox*) that forms a mound of honey-scented blooms.

white

White brings a calming and refreshing note to colours that are becoming increasingly brilliant.

There is a positive bonanza of white flowers in this season. Trees to create clouds of white blossom include snowy mespilus (*Amelanchier*) and many flowering cherries and crab apples, along with fruiting apples, plums, pears and cherries. Classiest and most opulent are the magnolias – substantial shrubs or small trees with huge, luxuriant blooms in goblet or star

creating strong contrasts in spring light

In spring the sun is still low in the sky and creates a soft light that moderates the intensity of bright colours. Now, brilliant shades can be used with impunity, for not only are they in keeping with the light, but the ephemeral nature of spring bulbs makes it possible to plant bold expanses of colour without a long-term commitment to such a scheme.

Tulips offer a particularly good range of bright colours and, with their long stems, they stand sentry-tall and straight above a carpet of spring bedding plants. They work wonderfully in containers as well as borders. Try bright yellow 'Golden Apeldoorn' over a carpet of yellow wallflowers (*Erysimum cheiri*), dark maroon 'Queen of Night' with pink or white pansies, or brilliant red tulips over a tapestry of white double daisies (*Bellis perennis*) and sky-blue forget-me-nots (*Myosotis*).

right: Tulips give an extra layer of colour over a carpet of spring bedding.

shapes that make a breathtaking display. Lovely though magnolias are, their sheer size and short flowering season confine their use to the larger garden, and there can be heartbreak when a late frost wreaks devastation on the flowers. More reliable are the fragrant lilacs (*Syringa vulgaris*), available in many shades but loveliest of all in whites such as 'Madame Lemoine'. Osmanthus species are strongly scented too but are less showy in appearance.

White climbers look gorgeous against a dark background. Twiners such as *Clematis montana* can scramble up a large holly or yew tree, while *Clematis armandii* creates its own backdrop with a mass of dark leathery leaves.

left: The large-flowered kingcup, *Caltha palustris* var. *palustris*.

blue

Blue continues to reflect the spring sky and is appearing in a continually increasing range of blooms.

Bulbs are the eyecatchers of the moment, creating glorious sheets of colour just about anywhere that there is a bit of space. The heavenly scented hyacinths go well in containers and formal bedding schemes, while the fairy bells of chionodoxa and scilla continue to bloom. Yet there is nothing to beat a mass of bluebells (*Hyacinthoides non-scripta*) carpeting the floor beneath trees whose just-opening leaves are the freshest of greens.

early summer

As the days lengthen and spring moves seamlessly into summer, the dominant colours of the garden become warmer and richer in tune with the strengthening rays of the sun. Now that the passionate explosion of spring colour has spent itself, the summer occupants begin to exert their influence with colours that are mostly soft and subtle, though with the occasional sparkling of roses and clematis in jewel-like shades as an overture to the brilliant colours that are soon to come. All the colours of early summer work well together in their pastel shades. When it comes to brighter shades, a little segregation into contrasting pairs is advisable, along with plenty of silver and grey foliage to act as a buffer.

above: Opium poppy (*Papaver somniferum*) is an easy annual to grow.

pink

Pink becomes more vibrant and sociable with the arrival of summer, compared to the ice-pinks and sugar-pinks of spring.

Alliums are summer-flowering bulbs that have a tremendous amount to offer, though too often they are forgotten in the rush to plant bulbs for spring. *Allium hollandicum* 'Purple Sensation' is one of the most striking, with large, rounded heads that look wonderful towering over Oriental poppies, particularly a variety in a complementary shade like the crushed-strawberry pink of *Papaver orientale* 'Patty's Plum'. In a cottage-garden-style border, peonies and the double-flowered *Aquilegia* 'Nora Barlow' make a delightful partnership. While *Clematis montana* varieties are still blooming well, the early large-flowered hybrid clematis begin to open their plate-sized blooms: 'Comtesse de Bouchaud' and 'Hagley Hybrid' are both interesting shades of pink.

yellow

Yellow, sunny and shining, enlivens plantings that could otherwise be just a little too soft.

The easy-growing nature of shrubs such as brooms (*Genista* and *Cytisus* species), and potentillas, along with a multitude of perennials – achilleas, coreopsis and irises to name but a few – makes it doubly enticing to plant lots of yellow, and there is a danger of overdoing this sunshine shade. However, as well as flowers, you should concentrate on foliage plants. Golden foliage looks especially fresh and lovely during this season, and serves so well as a backdrop to flowers and foliage in other colours. Climbers like the golden hop (*Humulus lupulus* 'Aureus') and *Jasminum officinale* 'Fiona Sunrise', the yellow-leaved form of summer jasmine, can be used to clothe walls and screens to make a backcloth of gold, while *Cornus alba* 'Aurea' (golden dogwood) is always excellent in borders.

blue

Blue now comes in a wealth of shades from pale mauve to rich purple blue.

The most enchanting blues of the season can be found among perennials and wall shrubs. Loveliest of all are the ceanothus. Sometimes called the californian liliac, these become covered in early summer with fluffy little heads in shades from palest ice blue to a sapphire so intense it can look unreal. While most types are wall shrubs, *C. thyrsiflorus* var. *repens* is a spreading variety, matched by the ground cover of *Lithodora diffusa* 'Heavenly Blue'. Pair these with the contrasting vertical stems of delphiniums and stunning bearded irises such as *Iris* 'Arabi Pasha'. Less intense but still lovely is catmint (*Nepeta* x *faassenii*), forming a low-down cloud of mauve flowers which is also lovely for planting beneath the tall lollipops of alliums.

silver

Silver looks its loveliest and most radiant in summer and is the perfect foil to many different flower colours.

Silver-grey foliage has an enchanting sparkle and freshness in early summer, although later on it can get dusty and tired. The finely cut leaves of artemisias and santolinas make a handsome contrast to bolder foliage and large flowers, and there are bold, gleaming shapes from the new leaves of biennials and perennials (see box). *Astelia chathamica* is especially deserving of a prime position to show off its wide, sword-shaped leaves.

making classic pastel combinations

Subtle and easy on the eye, pastel-coloured flowers with silver and grey foliage make a pleasing and restful combination. For the best results, do not mix every one of the colours of early summer but confine yourself to two colours plus foliage. Try pale pink and blue, creamy yellow and blue, pink and white, or blue and white.

The danger of such combinations is that they can appear soft and almost 'mushy' unless some strong structural elements are introduced. These can be found in bold plants such as cardoons (*Cynara cardunculus*), Scotch thistle (*Onopordum nervosum*), *Salvia argentea* and verbascums.

left: Tall delphiniums need plenty of care but are worth it for their azure-blue flower spikes.

below: Dutch irises, such as 'Golden Harvest' are an ideal way of enlivening dark areas in spring.

colour through the year 95

midsummer

Hot days quicken the tempo of the garden's colours, and now some of the most **vibrant** hues burst on to the scene. Brilliant, **jewel-like** colours glimmer against a background of green that has now matured to darker shades. However, there are still paler and pastel shades aplenty for those who prefer the summer garden to be softer and more subtle.

Roses are the flower of the moment and offer a wealth of **sumptuous** blooms in just about every colour except blue. And midsummer is when some short-lived but **spectacular** seasonal flowers take centre-stage with alacrity. Lovers of the low-maintenance garden may turn their noses up at the sowing and planting of annuals and tender perennials, but they pack an absolutely **unbeatable** punch of summer colour.

above: Silky-petalled *Eschscholzia californica.*

red

Red is hot and dramatic, glowing jewel-like in shades from flame to ruby and vermilion. The most sumptuous reds of the season belong to roses, and what a choice there is. Even better, many of the loveliest red roses are strongly perfumed too. Formal-looking hybrid tea roses such as 'Glad Tidings' and 'Royal William' look best grown in a bed dedicated to roses, with perhaps just a few perennials around their feet, while shrub roses such as 'Charles de Mills' and 'L.D. Braithwaite' make better mixers and can mingle in a border with other plants. Groundcover roses can be used on border edges or tumbling down banks ('Suffolk' and 'Flower Carpet Velvet' are both rewarding), and climbers such as 'Climbing Ena Harkness' and 'Etoile de Hollande' are perfect for walls, fences and screens.

orange

Orange is warm and friendly, and at its most enchanting during the long summer days. Vivid orange looks its best in bright sunlight, and most of the best orange flowers belong to sun-loving seasonal plants: pot marigolds (*Calendula*) in both single and double forms, Californian poppies (*Eschscholzia*), and gazanias are all available in clear, brilliant orange. *Mimulus aurantiacus* (shrubby musk) is a tender shrub in a slightly softer orange that is lovely for borders or containers. Dahlias and crocosmias, in shades ranging from soft apricot through clear orange to bronze-gold are now starting to bloom and often continue their fiery display through into autumn.

pink

Pink becomes increasingly warm and lively in its deepest shades but is a sociable mixer in its paler tones.

New or old, bush or climbing, every type of rose comes in an abundance of pinks. These range from palest blush such as *Rosa* 'Madame Alfred Carrière' through the silvery pink of 'New Dawn' to the rich deep pink of 'Gertrude Jekyll'.

Pink abounds in many other flowers too. Shrubs include the fast-growing and amenable

lavatera (tree mallow) varieties such as 'Barnsley' and 'Bredon Springs', *Buddleja* 'Pink Delight', which is the largest-flowered of all buddlejas, and the aptly named sun roses (*Cistus*) adore a hot, dry position. *C.* x *skanbergii* looks like a small dog rose, while the larger flowers of *C.* x *purpureus* are almost magenta. Frost-tender perennials include many diascias, geraniums, fuchsias, petunias and verbenas, plus lilies such as 'Stargazer' and Pink Perfection Group.

white

White is cool, tranquil and refreshing, just what you need on a hot, sultry day.

Many of the most elegant seasonal flowers are white and are lovely to use around parts of the garden where you sit, or that will be used in the evening as they remain visible long after all other colours have disappeared from view. Informal-looking flowers that can be popped into any gaps in the border include spider flower (*Cleome*), cosmos, gypsophila, annual mallow (*Lavatera* 'Mont Blanc') and African daisies (*Osteospermum*). Neater, low-growing ones with abundant flowers, like nemesia and sutera, are excellent in containers. A few have the bonus of a delectable scent, notably tobacco plant (*Nicotiana*) and several lilies, especially *Lilium regale*.

above: *Rosa* 'Madame Gregoire Staechelin'.

summer combinations for containers

Summer is the best time to experiment with all sorts of colour combinations, for this is when there is a wealth of seasonal flowers and foliage to play about with. First envisage where you would like to place your containers, then plant with the background as a complement or contrast. Here are a few ideas to try:

Soft pastels:
Pale pink trailing fuchsias such as 'Pink Marshmallow', pale pink ivy-leaved geraniums such as 'L'Elegante', trailing *Lobelia erinus* 'Blue Cascade' and variegated ground ivy (*Glechoma hederacea* 'Variegata').

Sunset shades:
Begonia 'Illumination Apricot' with bright yellow *Calceolaria* and orange and yellow trailing nasturtiums.

Symphony in pink:
Rosa 'Flower Carpet' underplanted with *Erigeron karvinskianus*, whose delicately pretty pink and white daisies will push up through every available space.

Regal violet and yellow:
Dwarf French marigolds with bushy or trailing blue *Lobelia erinus*.

White sophistication:
Lilies such as *Lilium* 'Kyoto' underplanted with a mass of white violas.

See pages 112–113 for more information on containers.

late summer

As the days imperceptibly begin to shorten, the garden takes on an air of **maturity**. Colours take on a **luminous** warmth, and the parchment yellows and browns of the first flower and seed heads weave their way among the still **abundant** flowers and foliage. The sun takes a lower passage across the sky and the garden looks **glorious** when backlit by the low rays of morning and evening. Now is the time to really crank up the **heat** with exotic-looking plants that have taken all summer to reach their full glory.

above: *Salvia patens* is the loveliest blue of all.

above: Gazanias are superb summer flowers.

blue

Blue takes on tones that are rich yet fresh, shading from mauve to indigo.

Deep, clear blues pack the greatest punch and make the best partners for bold colour contrasts. The tender perennial *Salvia patens* is the loveliest blue of all and well worth planting every year, while the deep azure blooms of *Ceratostigma willmottianum* and powder-puff clusters of *Ceanothus* x *delileanus* 'Topaze' are also outstanding. The spidery-petalled indigo-blue *Clematis* x *durandii* looks glorious with silver foliage. Butterflies flock to hebes, lavenders, the hyacinth-scented *Clematis heracleifolia* and, of course, the butterfly bush, *Buddleja davidii*.

green

Much striking and dramatic green foliage looks its best in late summer.

By late summer many spectacular foliage plants have reached their full glory. Tender plants such as bananas (*Musa* and *Ensete* species), cannas and the saw-leaved *Melianthus major* have large leaves that look wonderful in their own right and make a marvellous contrast to exotic-looking flowers. These tender plants combine well with permanent sword or dagger-like leaves of cordylines, phormiums and yuccas. For a touch of high drama, grow the foxglove tree (*Paulownia tomentosa*) and cut it back to the ground every spring, allowing just one stem to develop, so that the leaves become absolutely massive.

In shade or semi-shade there is plenty of lush foliage now too, thriving out of the sun's rays that would otherwise scorch their delicate leaves. King of them all is the tree fern *Dicksonia antarctica*, the trunk of which grows so, so slowly yet the giant fronds unfurl with almost watchable speed in spring. Underplant this statuesque beauty with smaller ferns like *Dryopteris filix-mas* (male fern) or *Polystichum aculeatum* (hard shield fern). Bamboos also thrive in shade and come in all sizes.

yellow

Glowing yellow flowers are joined now by the bleached shades of seed heads and the first hints of autumn leaf colour.

A host of summer yellows come from easy and reliable plants, such as shrubby potentillas spangled with little buttercup-like flowers, the button-like blooms of santolina, bold daisies of *Brachyglottis* (Dunedin Group) 'Sunshine' and the golden saucers of *Hypericum* 'Hidcote'. Bright bursts of seasonal flowers are supplied by many argyranthemums (marguerites), bidens and gazanias, exotic cannas, exuberant dahlias and late roses.

purple

Rich, opulent purples look most at home in late summer, among the sumptuous abundance of the year's growth.

Purple is regal and splendid and worth thought as to how it is placed. Use clematis to twine through shrubs and climbers whose moment of glory has passed, to spangle their staid foliage with jewel-like blooms. Varieties like *Clematis* 'Etoile Violette' or the rosette-shaped *C. viticella* 'Purpurea Plena Elegans' grow vigorously yet do not overwhelm their hosts. Or drape swags of a large-flowered clematis like 'Jackmanii Superba' along walls or trellis. The darkest and richest shades need a light background – silver foliage or a cream-painted wall – to show off their splendour; deep mauve forms marry well with clear light blue. Not all purples are emphatic: run drifts of *Verbena bonariensis* liberally through a border and its little lavender-like flowers borne on tall, airy stems will subtly unify the planting.

Purple foliage looks splendid now its full maturity has been reached. Dark-leaved forms of shrubs such as smoke bush (*Cotinus*), physocarpus and elder (*Sambucus*) create bold accent points throughout the border, while perennials like heucheras, *Saxifraga* 'Black Ruby' and purple-leaved ajugas infill on the ground.

creating exotic effects

A taste of the tropics need be no further away than your own back door if you use lush plants that have huge, dramatic leaves, eye-catching shapes and colours, and flowers in sizzling shades. Many sensational, tropical-style plants happily grow outdoors in colder areas and can be used to create a stunning display from early summer until the first frosts of autumn.

Choose a selection of dramatic green foliage plants as a backdrop for flamboyant seasonal flowers such as cannas, cleomes (spider flowers) and dahlias as well as the striking *Begonia* 'Dragon Wing'. Plant trailing golden bidens and hot-coloured petunias to weave a tapestry of colour over the ground. Narrow your colour choice a little to avoid an over-lurid planting: choose reds and oranges for a fiery appearance, with a splash of yellow if you wish, or hot pinks and purples for a darker and more sultry display.

below: Lush foliage plants create dramatic and exotic effects.

autumn

The garden gathers itself for a final **fiery** pageant of colour, almost in defiance of the coming winter that will inevitably extinguish the **blaze**. Late-blooming perennials join forces with a plethora of **vibrantly coloured** fruits and berries, while falling night temperatures bring about a startling change in many trees and shrubs that, almost overnight, it seems, take on the **gorgeous** autumn mantles of oranges, scarlets, golds and russets. The shades of autumn are some of the **richest** and loveliest of all, and are never more glorious than when viewed against a heavenly deep blue sky.

above: Fiery colour from red hot pokers (*Kniphofia*).

yellow

Golden foliage, as well as gleaming yellow flowers, brighten the shortening days.

Late flowers in radiant golden yellows lift the spirits like nothing else. Grow *Clematis tangutica* and *C. tibetana* subsp. *vernayi* on trellis and pergolas, where the nodding, lantern-shaped flowers can be seen outlined against the blue sky. In borders, heleniums, chrysanthemums and rudbeckias create pools of gold among rich autumn greens and colourful leaves or flowers. Yellow fruits and berries stand out against green foliage. Many of the best berry-bearing trees and shrubs include yellow-fruiting varieties, such as *Pyracantha* 'Saphyr Jaune', *Malus* x *zumi* 'Golden Hornet' and *Cotoneaster salicifolius* 'Rothschildianus'.

Maples are famed for their autumn colouring and *Acer cappadocicum* and *A. rufinerve* have large leaves that turn butter-yellow; the small leaves of birch (*Betula*) look like golden pennies; and the golden-leaved false acacia, *Robinia pseudacacia* 'Frisia', turns from lime-yellow to rich old-gold.

orange

Orange is marmalade and bronze, amber and ginger in its autumn tones, joyful but not garish in this season.

Orange is a key colour of many autumn foliage plants that make a truly spectacular show. These include many maples and berberis, snowy mespilus (*Amelanchier*), *Fothergilla* and the lit-by-fire *Parrotia persica*. Orange fruit and berries are also plentiful, from crab apples such as *Malus* 'John Downie' to pyracanthas and the spiny *Poncirus trifoliata* (bitter orange). *Iris foetidissima* bursts its seed heads to reveal the big shining beads hidden within. Link different plants together with bronze-flowered varieties of that quintessential autumn flower, the chrysanthemum.

red

Red abounds in many flowers, as well as in fruits and autumn leaves.

Late-blooming reds continue to delight, particularly the superb seasonal performers such as *Cosmos atrosanguineus*, dahlias and salvias in glowing shades. But the best reds are from those plants that cloak themselves in autumn fire when their leaves turn colour before falling. The most brilliant include the smoke bush (*Cotinus*) and spindle bush *Euonymus europaeus* 'Red Cascade'. The purplish leaves of *Sambucus nigra* 'Guincho Purple' and *Vitis vinifera* 'Purpurea' turn

brilliant scarlet among their purple-black fruit. Many rowans (*Sorbus*) and most cotoneasters also have brilliant berries, and don't forget rosehips: those on *Rosa rugosa* are large and fat, and *R.* 'Geranium' puts on a terrific show with its flagon-shaped hips.

pink

Vivid pink makes a startling contrast but one that is not out of place with the glowing colours of the season.

Autumn-flowering bulbs provide some wonderfully lurid bubblegum-pinks, particularly *Amaryllis belladonna* and *Nerine bowdenii*. While their large flowers have a tendency to sit uneasily in a mixed border, these bulbs look best when planted in broad ribbons at the base of a sunny wall to make a spectacular show of bloom. Better for mixing with other plants are kaffir lilies (*Schizostylis coccinea* 'Mrs Hegarty' is a lovely clear shade), which will bloom into winter if the weather is kind. Brighten shady spots with the dainty and tough little autumn-flowering *Cyclamen hederifolium*, which carries on to give extra interest with marbled leaves. All these pinks make an astonishingly effective picture pushing up through the flame colours of fallen leaves.

below: The autumn-flowering bulb *Nerine bowdenii*.

autumn fruits and berries

Colourful fruits and berries often receive little consideration when planning a planting, but they give colour for a much longer period than flamboyant but short-lived autumn foliage. Red and orange fruits are the most popular with birds and tend to disappear first, so it is worth planting some trees and shrubs with longer-lasting yellow, white or pink berries, such as *Cotoneaster* x *watereri* 'Pink Champagne', *Malus* x *zumi* 'Golden Hornet' and *Sorbus hupehensis*.

For extra impact before winter closes in, choose plants with both colourful fruit and

autumn leaves. Both the tiny leaves and the berries of the fishbone cotoneaster (*Cotoneaster horizontalis*) turn glowing red, and the mountain ash (*Sorbus aucuparia*) is always eye-catching with its butter-yellow autumn leaves and trusses of scarlet berries. If the weather is kind you will be treated to a wonderful few days when the plant is surrounded by a circlet of golden fallen leaves while the fruit remains on the tree.

left: *Sedum spectabile* with the dangling flowers of a red fuchsia.

winter

Winter is less a season for creating colour schemes than for just creating colour of any sort to **brighten** the gloom. Yet, despite the harsh weather, there are still plants that **brave** the conditions to look good right though until spring, with attractive foliage, long-lasting berries, **colourful** stems and a few winter flowers. Place these plants where they can be seen from indoors or at least where you will see them every day, in order to enjoy their winter beauty to the full.

Winter also offers the chance for the garden to give beauty in more subtle ways. Once autumn's magnificence has come to a close, do not hasten to tidy up the garden. Delay cutting back perennials and ornamental grasses until late winter or early spring and you will be able to enjoy the **ethereal** beauty of bare stems and leaf skeletons when rimed and **silvered** with frost. On a down-to-earth practical note, plants and useful insects both benefit from the extra winter cover.

above: Long-lasting berries provide welcome winter colour.

red

Bright, sealing-wax red survives in many stems and berries, bringing a festive touch to the winter garden. Red berries and stems make a stunning contrast to rich green foliage. While many red fruits attract birds, some others, including *Crataegus persimilis* 'Prunifolia' and *Malus* x *robusta* 'Red Sentinel', last through the winter. Skimmias and *Gaultheria procumbens* are well worth making room for, as they combine lustrous evergreen foliage with showy red berries, giving a superb show for months. The red stems of *Cornus alba*, revealed after the leaves have fallen, gain extra lustre now, particularly when caught in the low winter sun.

green

Green foliage looks rich and striking against bare brown earth and naked stems. Evergreen foliage is the mainstay of the garden and steps out to take centre stage this season, when most other plants have died back or shed their leaves. Bold shapes and textures create plenty of much-needed structural interest too. Choose plants that are naturally architectural in habit, such as mahonias or spiky-leaved phormiums and yuccas, and shapely conifers and hollies. Alternatively, endow nondescript plants with personality by clipping privet, box and yew into attractive and striking shapes.

gold

Gold seems to capture and hold the rare winter sunshine within the garden.

Golden or green-and-yellow foliage shrubs bring a welcome touch of permanent winter sunshine and are always worth planting. Aucubas, elaeagnus, euonymus and hollies can all be found in many variegated varieties. These useful plants are all too often neglected but contribute tremendously to the winter garden. Conifers come in to their own this season, too, with many shades of gold. Some maintain the same bright gold all year, while others such as *Thuja occidentalis* 'Rheingold' and *T. orientalis* 'Amber Queen' turn deeper bronze in winter. There is a handful of yellow winter-flowering plants too, chief of which is *Jasminum nudiflorum* (winter jasmine) – a tough, easy and beautiful wall shrub that no garden should be without. Mahonias, which are invaluable for their bold leaves, are always a surprise when their lily-of-the-valley scented yellow flowers suddenly appear in late winter.

white

White, echoing snow and frost, and is found in many winter flowers.

Many enchantingly fragile winter blooms are white, blush or cream, looking like snow that has fallen and decided to stay. Sometimes a little cosseting is necessary. The Christmas rose (*Helleborus niger*) will benefit from the protection of glass or cloches so the large petals remain unsullied by harsh weather. Others, though, are reassuringly tough: winter-flowering heathers, Christmas box (*Sarcococca*), laurustinus (*Viburnum tinus*), *Viburnum* x *bodnantense* and the shrubby winter-flowering honeysuckle (*Lonicera* x *purpusii* 'Winter Beauty' is one of the best). While severe weather may set back one crop of flowers, invariably more appear once the weather picks up again, and all except the heathers have the most delicious scent. And, last but not least, the snowdrops open to show that spring isn't too far away.

White-stemmed plants look most striking of all against the dark background of a winter garden. The white-barked birches *Betula utilis* var. *jacquemontii* and 'Silver Shadow' make a classic winter combination when underplanted with a circle of colourful winter-flowering heathers. For a wild or woodland garden, the grey-white stems of *Rubus thibetanus* (ghost bramble) stand out among the bare branches and dark leaves.

below: Evergreen foliage and winter flowers make *Viburnum tinus* an essential garden plant.

colourful winter foliage

Evergreens are the stalwarts of the winter garden, revealing their true value when all else has died back. While it's tempting to opt for lots of bright yellow foliage, too much, even in winter, can make the garden looking brassy and even a little sick. Concentrate on greens for your winter backbone, choosing different tones of green such as dark *Viburnum davidii* and *Osmanthus*, rich green *Chamaecyparis lawsoniana* 'Green Hedger' and bronze-tinged *Juniperus communis* 'Hornibrookii'. A small handful of worthwhile plants develop deeper and more intense colours as the temperature falls: *Chamaecyparis thyoides* 'Ericoides' turns from green to rusty brown, and *Hebe* 'Red Edge' and 'Sweet Kim' that have glaucous foliage that becomes strongly tinged with pink.

below: Evergreen *Euonymus* with coloured dogwood stems and pink *Daphne mezereum*.

outdoor decorating

boundaries

Every garden needs boundaries, so it makes sense to turn these edges into something far more than functional, to make a great **decorative** contribution to the garden. All but the tiniest plots benefit from internal screens or dividers too, in order to hide practical or unsightly features. Coloured wood stains are perfect for **revitalizing** fences and there is a wealth of masonry paints to **transform** walls. Specialist paint suppliers offer eco-friendly products, lime-based paint that is designed to weather with age, and paint with a chalky finish.

A boundary is likely to cover a large area so it is important to choose the right shade if you wish to use colour on it. While bright colours are striking and can make an exceptional design statement, bear in mind that they may look overpowering over a large area and may also look outdated within a relatively short space of time. If you are opting for a vivid shade such as orange or purple, select plants in a very limited selection of complementary colours that will be shown off to the best advantage against such a bold background.

Subtle colours are easier and complement a wide selection of plants. The safest choices are soft orange and yellow, bluish pink, pale blue and silver-grey. Green may appear to be another obvious safe choice, but many shades tend to work less successfully than might be expected, simply because their tones can be too close to those of the plants themselves.

For a completely natural look that never fails to make a handsome backdrop to a planting, go for screens made of materials such as bamboo, willow, peeled reed or heather. Most of these are sold inexpensively as rolls or, a more costly option, as individual framed panels. Rolled screening is a brilliant way of covering up an ugly fence that belongs to your neighbour – simply fix it in place with U-shaped staples for an instant transformation.

practicalities

When painting a fence, bear in mind that both sides will need treating – not only to keep the wood in good condition, but also because drips of stain will run through the other side. If the fence belongs to your neighbour, do check with them first before starting work. Roll-on stains make fast work of treating large areas, although the range of colours available in this form is limited.

left: Basement gardens need never be gloomy. Go for muted shades such as this blue-green, which appears to recede, rather than bright colours that would make the wall seem to come forward. Harmony is vital in such a limited space where lots of clutter would make the area appear even smaller and here a selection of galvanized planters and accessories cleverly contrasts, but not too starkly, with the wall.

above: A rich terracotta backdrop transforms what could so easily be a rather suburban-looking raised bed. This earthy colour looks outstanding with plants, particularly as it has been put on as a thin 'wash' so glimpses of the lighter base show through. This is more effective than if applied as a solid colour, where the effect might overpower the planting.

right: Stained in soft blue, this close-board fence becomes an integral part of the border colour scheme, rather than a separate and purely functional backdrop. Such a colourful background needs careful thought as to the plant colours in the border. All-white, or cream and purple would have been restrained choices, but these more adventurous yellows and purples are successful because of the limited palette and the use of plenty of green as a buffer. Note the slender bamboo wigwams painted in darker blue that create instant height within the planting.

verticals

Vertical features literally create a whole new **dimension** in a garden; they also give a huge amount of visual interest and provide more growing space for plants. Arches, arbours, pergolas, trellis and obelisks can be used in many different sites around the garden, no matter how small or large the plot may be. Such features can serve a practical purpose, too. A pergola will cast an **enticing**, dappled shade over a sun-baked patio, and a little arbour or summerhouse will make a peaceful spot in which to relax. Smaller verticals can transform mundane areas – consider putting an archway over a front gate or a series of arches over a long path.

The very nature of the different styles of all these verticals can make for a disparate overall appearance in the garden, but harmony can be easily restored simply by using coloured stain or paint to introduce an overall colour scheme. If there are more than a couple of features that are given the colour treatment, you may like to introduce variety by combining two closely related and complementary shades, such as medium and dark blue. A timber arbour, for example, could have its walls and roof painted mid-blue with the framework picked out in a darker shade. Other combinations that work well include dark green with a lighter shade of silver-green, and blue with ash-grey highlights.

Climbing plants are likely to be scrambling cheek by jowl with many vertical features, so bear these colour partnerships in mind when choosing both paint and plants – many of the same considerations apply to vertical features as to boundaries (see page 106). While flowers attract the greatest attention and make superb seasonal highlights, the longest-lasting and most decorative colour schemes are achieved by using climbers with attractive foliage. Try golden hop or ivy against a blue background, for example, or silver grey as a backdrop to *Parthenocissus henryana*, with its pewter-veined leaves and deep claret undersides.

above: Vivid colours bring an air of theatre into the garden. Working to a colour theme by coordinating features and planting is essential when using bright colours – just visualize how out of place the purple trellis would be without the complementary planting of pink and purple flowers at its base. Ultra-bright schemes such as these tend to look best close to the house, rather than surrounded by planting further down the garden.

left: Free-standing plant supports are outstanding for creating instant height within a border. Away from the house and surrounded by plants, softer and natural colours are by far the best option. At present the effect here is architectural – a gold and green skirt of tulips and variegated holly around the base of the bare obelisk – but in time the climbing plants will transform the whole feature into a pillar of foliage and flowers.

above: First impressions are all-important, yet garden entrances rarely receive the attention they deserve. Colour-coordinating several different vertical elements creates a marvellous feeling of unity that entices the visitor through the gate and up the path. This single hoop arch, the same colour and shape as the doorway beyond, gives the impression of walking through a 'magical archway' as you enter the garden.

right: Trellis is excellent in many situations; as a garden divider, on boundaries, or to screen off unsightly objects. the combination of broad slats and abundant planting gives privacy, yet without the claustrophobic effect that can be created by a solid fence. Stained in deep, dark shades, trellis makes the perfect support for rich red, climbing roses and clematis, and a handsome backdrop to purple and pink flowers that include *Lavatera* and *Achillea*.

practicalities

Timber features need particular attention where the sections are in direct contact with the ground, as the damp conditions make the wood more liable to rot in time. Check when you buy the wood that it has been pressure-treated with preservative. For extra protection, also dip the post ends in preservative and allow them to dry thoroughly before putting up the structure.

the garden floor

The surfaces within a garden are central to its SUCCeSS, setting an overall style and creating the very **bones** of the design, much as the choice of flooring inside can dictate the entire look and feel of a room.

The patio is usually the largest hard area within the garden and has a hugh influence both indoors and out. Elsewhere, paths and steps dictate how people move through the garden, so both shape and material should be chosen with care.

Hard surfaces usually cost a lot of money and are intended to last for years, so it is vital to plan their colour, size and layout with care and to build them properly. Take account of the other surrounding hard surfaces, such as house walls – the material should blend in with them. Choose the material as you would a carpet, by bringing home samples of different materials to compare *in situ*.

A patio surface needs to unite the house and garden, so this colour choice needs the greatest consideration of all. Paving comes in a huge range of sizes and finishes, mostly in natural shades. As with boundaries, subtle and

natural colours are the easiest to work with. Timber decking can be stained in a range of colours, but be sure to choose a hard-wearing stain that is designed especially for this purpose, as well as a sealant to keep out the damp. Decking is particularly useful for tackling awkward sites such as sloping ground, as the underlying framework can be made to fit tricky contours.

Patios are always the focus for outdoor living, but elsewhere in the garden, labour-intensive lawns can be replaced by materials that are hard-wearing, need very little attention, and stay smart for years. Doing

away with the lawn entirely is a practical option in small gardens where a tiny area of grass quickly becomes worn and tatty.

The same low-maintenance principle can be extended into planted areas by covering bare soil with a hard mulch such as gravel or chippings, chosen to complement the planting and surrounding features. Choose from natural gravel, stone or slate chippings, or recycled glass made into 'gravel' – this also comes in bright colours suited to a modern garden. Gravel or chippings are also a better option for very shady areas where other hard materials tend to become slimy with algae.

practicalities

For loose surfaces such as gravel, chippings and bark to look good for years with little maintenance they must be laid on top of permeable membrane, a landscaping fabric that suppresses weed growth while still letting water through. Then, lay the top surface in a layer 5cm (2in) thick.

above: Stone setts make a very appropriate path through a gently disordered, cottage-style planting. This is not a style of dramatic contrasts, and the soft colour is just right for offsetting and giving form to the foam of summer flowers. Small-unit paving in natural colours is a good choice for tiny gardens as it creates the impression of greater space.

left: More than just a path, this blue gravel creates a stream-like effect through a tapestry of planting that sparkles in jewel-like colours. It has greater impact than a mown grass path and is a more imaginative feature than a seat. The colour is a clever choice: distinctive but not too harsh, and an effective counterpoint to the myriad flower colours.

right: Go for the Mediterranean look with terracotta tiles. This earthy shade suits a great number of colour schemes, and the blue edges and insets used here help link the tiling with the silver, blues and soft purples that billow up either side. Straight edges benefit from being softened with plants, here by the lacy silver foliage of *Artemisia* 'Powis Castle'.

containers

Gone are the days when the choices for containers were limited to terracotta, wood, stone or hideous white plastic. Now there is not only a **fantastic** choice of pots in many different materials and a wide range of colours, but good **quality** outdoor paints make an effective job of **transforming** almost anything from wooden tubs to throwaway items recycled as planters. Pots can create an instant garden and juggling the display from time to time will give a new look in minutes.

If you already have a mixture of containers, introduce some harmony by separating them into groups of the same material and put each group in a different part of the garden. Alternatively, paint them in unifying colours. Personalize plain, cheap, terracotta pots with your own designs, first applying a primer and then a coloured emulsion. Simple designs stencilled on with spray paint look lovely against a plain background.

From a planting point of view, containers are unbeatable for colour right through the year. Start in spring with a succession of different bulbs to provide months of vivid colour. The best for containers are crocus, hyacinths, narcissi (small and multi-headed types last much longer than trumpet-flowered daffodils) and tulips (hybrids rather than species). For summer there is an immense choice of flowering annuals and tender perennials, from trailing bidens, scaevola and sutera to stately cannas, while diascias, fuchsias, gazanias, nemesias and pelargoniums are all rewarding in containers. Ornamental grasses and herbaceous perennials with decorative foliage provide a handsome backdrop. Autumn stars such as chrysanthemums, dahlias, Miracle Series cyclamen and *Erica gracilis* bloom for months until the frosts, and look superb with foliage plants such as ivies along with ornamental cabbages and kale. Evergreens come into their own for winter, particularly those with colourful or rich green foliage.

Containers also make great guinea-pigs for experimenting with all kinds of colour schemes – simply shift the pots around to test out different combinations. Once you hit upon a favourite colour scheme, adapt it for larger areas of the garden too.

left: Brightly coloured glazed pots look even better when the compost is hidden by gleaming glass 'gravel' – here the uninterrupted deep blue creates a striking contrast with the green palm foliage. The gravel serves a practical purpose too, by reducing water loss and preventing rain-splashed soil dirtying the pot. Glazed pots are particularly good where sun is in short supply, not only for their intrinsic brightness but also because their shiny surfaces reflect the light.

right: Sophisticated and subtle, these galvanized pots make a superb complement to the silver and blue-grey foliage and white flowers. This grouping is saved from being just too tasteful by the contrasting purple foliage behind, picked up by the purple-flushed sempervivums clustered around the feet of the pots. Containers look far better in groups, so choose colours and materials that harmonize.

below: Sleek, modern containers are perfect for hostas and purple heucheras with bold foliage. Orange geums make a striking contrast. Lots of small plants with fussy, little leaves would not work so well, but they can make useful foils to the more striking plants.

above: A few pots of paint and some old oil drums make it possible to have a great-looking potted garden for next to nothing. Any item that can hold compost and have drainage holes made in the base can be transformed into a plant container, and the most unpromising materials can be revamped to bring life and colour to a small urban garden.

practicalities
Top tips for successful containers

- Ensure all containers have drainage holes and put pieces of polystyrene, stones or broken pots in the base so water drains freely.

- Used containers should be washed first as pests and diseases can lurk in debris.

- Always use fresh potting compost.

- Regular watering is vital and plants may need watering up to twice a day in sunny, breezy weather.

- Avoid watering in the heat of the day when water splashes can cause scorching.

- Feeding is necessary during the growing season as the fertilizer in compost becomes used up after about six weeks.

- Deadhead flowering plants every few days for the best performance.

finishing touches

The greatest fun and flexibility can be found in the finishing touches within a garden, which provide the perfect way to stamp your own personality on your plot. The possibilities are limitless, so start by deciding on the overall look that you'd like to create – taking inspiration from the inside of your house, as described on page 6, is a good place to begin. First of all, choose practical additions such as garden furniture, move on to design essentials to create focal points (see below), and then complete the picture with some individual touches to add a bit of zing around the garden.

Browsing through garden centres, department stores and garden shows will turn up a vast selection of garden decorations, yet there are far more sources of potential 'ornaments'. Yesterday's junk is often today's fashion, and a search through second-hand shops and reclamation yards can yield a rich harvest. Let your imagination run wild and see how items such as discarded tables and chairs, or old kitchen utensils, could be incorporated into a planting scheme. A coat of paint can transform sad, battered pieces into striking, contemporary garden ornaments, so take a close look at anything that can be given the colour treatment and is suitable for outdoor use. Or, if you're at all handy at woodwork, you could turn your hand to making your own garden features such as simple benches or border edges.

Whatever style you opt for, placement is all important. Identify the focal points around your garden that would benefit from highlighting with some form of decoration. These are the centre points of the key views from your house windows and the patio and other seating areas, as well as viewpoints that are revealed on a walk around the garden. Ring the changes from year to year with different colours on items that are easy to paint. There are paints to suit almost any material, not just wood. Consider adding more detail and decorative effect by techniques such as stencilling or colour-washing, too.

left: Steps must be functional and safe, but there is no reason for them not to be decorative as well. Make the most of the untrodden areas at the sides with ornaments such as this imaginative collection of spheres, which creates a contrast of shape as well as colour. Pots of plants can also be employed to cheer up a dull set of steps, but make sure they don't make the tread area too narrow.

right: Permanent garden furniture will make an obvious place to pause – to relax, sit, talk or eat. Make sure that its size is in proportion to the garden as furniture shouldn't overwhelm the available space. A number of different colours might have been chosen for the table and chairs in this rooftop garden, but natural colours and neutrals provide a smart, classic look that will never date.

below: A plain garden bench is transformed from understudy into star with a coat of bright paint and a couple of pots of begonias burgeoning with apricot-coloured blooms. Bring about a yearly transition with a simple piece of furniture such as this that is quick and easy to paint.

right: The shimmering qualities of this mosaic wall create a semi-exotic backdrop to a border of fragrant plants that includes catmint, lavender, and the striped Bourbon rose 'Ferdinand Pichard'. Harmony is everything – without the sumptuous blue glazed pots to echo the mosaic colour, it could look rather out of place. Mosaics need not just be of this classic design; make your own using broken pieces of colourful kitchen plates.

planting

planting your garden

While it is hugely tempting to leap straight into buying and planting, it pays to keep a cool head and do a little planning. First, make a detailed assessment of your garden, then move on to the really fun part – working out your own colour schemes. Follow the checklists and guidance through this chapter and you'll find that creating a garden becomes approachable, fun, and ultimately hugely rewarding.

garden assessment

Draw up a rough sketch plan of your garden, mark on the permanent fixtures such as walls, fences, paths and any large plants you wish to keep, and then consider the following:

● Which parts of the garden receive most sun and which are mostly shady? How does this vary with the seasons? (See pages 76–79.)

● Does your soil dry out quickly, stay waterlogged, or is it a happy balance? Does it vary in different parts of the garden? Check your soil type and the pH, which may influence the plants you choose. (See pages 80–81.)

● Are parts of the garden exposed to wind and will need tough, hardy plants and possibly a windbreak? Are there warm, sheltered spots that would suit plants on the borderline of hardiness? Low-lying areas tend to be more subject to frost.

● Colour can be amazingly effective in creating the illusion of space. (See pages 82–83.) Where would this be helpful?

● Where in the garden would you most value colour in the winter? And in the summer? In the evenings? (See pages 78–79)

● Are there any areas of the garden that are used at specific times of day? Some flowers close up when the sun is not on them, while others are at their best in the evening.

● What permanent backdrops do you have to work with? Note the colour of buildings and walls that cannot be changed, and take into account the colour of existing hedges and large plants.

As you make notes you will probably find new ideas forming in your mind. Jot them down.

shape, texture and habit

Colour is never seen in isolation in a garden, for our perception of colour is hugely influenced by the **shape** and **texture** of stems, leaves and flowers. We have seen how a glossy green varies from a matt, felted green, how airy panicles appear quite different from bold, solid petals of the same colour. Imagine a planting that is carefully colour-themed but with no variation of shape – the result would be hideously monotonous. When planning planting groups, you can create **striking** effects by partnering fragile leaves or flowers with large or coarsely textured foliage, and vice versa. For example, a hazy cloud of delicate gypsophila makes a dynamic **contrast** to the corrugated leaves of *Viburnum davidii*. Conversely, put big blooms like those of peonies and *Echinacea purpurea* next to feathery fennel (*Foeniculum vulgare*) or soft-needled conifers.

left: The formal pyramid shapes of box (*Buxus sempervirens*) are ideal for year-round structure.

As well as using leaves and flowers of differing forms, consider the variety of overall shapes or habits. Grouping plants of contrasting habits will add enormously to the final effect. Although a rounded habit predominates among plants, there are many other interesting outlines:

● **Vertical:** bamboos (many varieties including *Fargesia murieliae*, *Phyllostachys*), crocosmias, irises, strong-stemmed ornamental grasses such as *Miscanthus sinensis*, plume poppy (*Macleaya cordata*).

● **Narrow and upright** (fastigiate)**:** *Berberis thunbergii* 'Helmond Pillar', many conifers such as *Juniperus scopulorum* 'Skyrocket', *Taxus baccata* 'Fastigiata', *Prunus* 'Amanogawa', *Malus* 'Van Eseltine' and *Sorbus aucuparia* 'Fastigiata'.

● **Spiky:** Agaves, *Astelia*, cordylines, phormiums, yucca.

● **Weeping or arching:** *Acer palmatum* 'Dissectum' varieties (Japanese maples), *Pyrus salicifolia* 'Pendula' (weeping silver pear), *Malus* 'Royal Beauty' (weeping crab apple), *Salix purpurea* 'Pendula' (weeping purple willow), *Prunus* x *yedoensis* 'Shidare Yoshino' (weeping cherry).

Certain plants may not be naturally architectural in habit, but they can have form imposed upon them. This need not be as extreme as with the art of topiary, by which plants such as box and yew are trimmed into all sorts of complex spirals, lollipops and animal shapes. It simply involves endowing an amenable plant with a little more shape and character than would occur if left to its own

devices. For example, tall plants such as holly (*Ilex*), golden privet (*Ligustrum ovalifolium* 'Aureum') and Italian buckthorn (*Rhamnus alaternus* 'Argenteovariegata') can be clipped into broad cones or pyramids, the shrubby honeysuckle *Lonicera nitida* 'Baggesen's Gold' and most *Osmanthus* make good dense domes, while small shrubs like lavender and santolina trim well into neat little mounds and can serve as small formal hedges. This is a great way to bring a little more shape and form to existing plants in your garden. Many shrubs can also be trained into standards – that is, a 'lollipop' shape with a rounded head of foliage on a clear stem.

With all the basic information on your site now to hand, you are ready to start drawing up your planting plan. It's far easier to make any mistakes on paper rather than after you have bought your plants.

above: The spiky foliage of ornamental grasses also brings an airy texture to planting.

left: A handsome combination of plants chosen for their contrasting shapes and textures, of flowers as well as foliage.

building up a scheme

Now you have an **overview** of your garden with all the necessary information, you can **indulge** in some colour scheming. Start with your **favourite** colour and decide whether you want a harmony of closely related colours or the more **dramatic** effect of colour contrasts. Look back at Your Garden Palette (see page 20) and Exploring Colour Combinations (se page 10) if you want a reminder of the best **plant partners** to choose. If you still can't make up your mind, try the technique for choosing combinations described on page 13.

right: A mixed group of different types of plant gives maximum colour and interest.

planning a planting

trees

As the largest plants of all, trees should be selected first. Those with green or softly coloured leaves are the safest bet – golds and purples will look very dominant as the trees grow larger. Consider the shape as well as how many seasons of interest it will provide.
Suggestions: *Amelanchier, Betula, Gleditsia, Malus, Sorbus.*

evergreen shrubs and conifers

If around a third of all the medium to large plants in the garden are evergreen you will have a good balance of plants giving year-round structure and long-lasting colour. Again, go easy on gold foliage unless you are creating a border with a definite yellow theme. Include some bold, architectural shapes.
Suggestions: *Aucuba, Berberis, Choisya, Elaeagnus, Euonymus, Fargesia, Fatsia, Mahonia, Phormium, Yucca,* conifers, *Chamaecyparis, Juniperus, Taxus, Thuja.*

deciduous shrubs for foliage

Shrubs with attractive foliage make a fantastic backdrop to flowers. Keep contrasts in mind, and choose specimens that will look good from spring to autumn.
Suggestions: *Cornus, Cotinus, Physocarpus, Sambucus.*

deciduous shrubs for flowers

Choose a mixture of flowering shrubs to give interest and colour at different times of year. Shrubs which have a second season of interest, with berries or bright autumn foliage, are especially good value.
Suggestions: *Abutilon, Buddleja, Caryopteris, Ceanothus, Exochorda, Forsythia, Lavatera, Potentilla, Rosa, Spiraea, Viburnum.*

infill plants

These should provide you with a succession of interesting foliage or flowers over a long period, and a limitless choice of colours.
Suggestions: *Ajuga, Alchemilla, Artemisia, Coreopsis, Dryopteris, Euphorbia, Hebe, Helleborus, Heuchera, Helenium, Iris, Stachys,* various grasses.

seasonal plants

Annuals, biennials and frost-tender perennials are all excellent value for summer and autumn colour. Bulbs can be planted in the spaces between groups of plants and to grow through carpets of ground cover.
Suggested annuals and tender perennials: *Bidens, Calendula, Cerinthe, Felicia, Mimulus, Nicotiana, Nigella, Scaevola.*
Suggested bulbs: *Chionodoxa, Crocus, Galanthus, Narcissus, Scilla, Tulipa*

climbers

Use these to cover walls, fences, arches and pergolas, and grow some of the less vigorous climbers through established trees and shrubs to create an extra garland of colour. Match a climber's vigour to that of its host.
Suggestions: *Akebia quinata, Clematis, Ipomoea tricolor, Jasminum officinale, Lonicera, Parthenocissus, Rosa.*

choosing your plants step-by-step

A blend of different types of plant gives the maximum colour choice and variety. Choose your plants with care to have something looking good every month of the year. Start by selecting plants for winter and early spring when colourful plants are scarce, then autumn, spring and summer – in that order.

key plants

The plants that will form the 'backbone' of your garden planting are primarily the medium-sized and large ones – shrubs, conifers and trees – and these should be chosen first of all. Because of their size these plants really need to pull their weight and look colourful for as long as possible. Try to see beyond the immediate appeal of flowers and instead look for attributes such as foliage with an attractive shape or colour, colourful bark, or two seasons of interest such as spring flowers followed by autumn fruit.

Place all these larger plants first, allowing plenty of room according to their eventual height and spread. Correctly spaced plants will look gappy at first but will fill out quickly.

infill planting

Once the backbone plants are placed, move on to the smaller ones like perennials, ornamental grasses, small shrubs and roses. While a few of these should have long-lasting attractive foliage – either evergreen or deciduous – or an architectural shape, many of these infill plants can be seasonal performers with shorter but showier bursts of colour. For the most part, place larger plants further back and grade down to the small ones towards the front, but it pays to have the occasional tall plant at the front so long as it has a light, airy habit.

safety in numbers

Unless the style of planting is distinctly formal, with a symmetrical layout and straight lines, the most effective way to set out plants is in drifts or long, irregular groups. Weave these drifts through the border, avoiding straight runs, to keep a relaxed and informal feel to the planting.

Although a border needs a variety of different plants to give plenty of interest, beware of seeking constant change. The most attractive effects are created by planting some repeated groups or drifts of the same plants, setting up a rhythm of colour that unifies and is easy on the eye.

above: Make the most of the available space by planting at every level, from the ground up. Restrict the number of colours for maximum effect – blue and white look wonderful here.

below: In between the key plants, infill with flowers for a mass of seasonal colour.

planting in layers

In a small garden or where you want to pack in more plants, achieve maximum colour from the available space by 'layering' together plants of different types in tiers.

1 Choose a tree that only casts a light, dappled shade like a birch or rowan, so there is a good choice of plants to go underneath.

2 Select a medium-sized shrub that thrives in dappled shade, such as spotted laurel (*Aucuba japonica* 'Crotonifolia'), dogwood (*Cornus alba* varieties), mock orange (*Philadelphus*) and viburnums.

3 Under the deciduous shrub, plant a carpet of low-growing, shade-tolerant plants that perform in winter or spring before the larger shrub leafs up. These include epidemiums, *Geranium phaeum*, hellebores, lungworts (*Pulmonaria*) and periwinkles (*Vinca minor*).

4 Between these low-growing plants, plant drifts of spring bulbs like crocus or narcissi.

5 After several years, when the larger plants have become well established, pack in even more colour by planting climbers to grow through these living supports. Well-behaved climbers that won't overwhelm their hosts include large-flowered hybrid clematis; *C. viticella* varieties, golden hop (*Humulus lupulus* 'Aureus') and perennial sweet pea (*Lathyrus latifolius*).

the cottage border

A romantic and colourful blend of flowers and fragrance is most people's idea of a cottage-style border. Originally the role of the cottage garden was a practical one, with herbs, fruit and vegetables taking priority over flowers. Now looks matter most, although good-looking edible plants can play a dual role.

When planning a cottage garden it is useful to think of it as a very informal version of a classic border in order to have sufficient long-lasting interest and colour. Give consideration to shape, texture and seasonal interest to avoid the pitfall of having lots of summer flowers with little to look at in other seasons.

While cottage style is often visualized as a jumble of colours, restricting the range to several complementary ones will look far better than a hotch-potch of different shades. Here the colour scheme revolves around pink and soft shades of yellow. A few red flowers add 'bite' to the scheme.

1 The brighter colours in this border are broken up by white and soft yellow, so the pinks and reds do not jar with each other.

2 Roses are a popular choice for a cottage border, preferably varieties with an old-fashioned appearance.

3 Fragrance is essential, from perfumed flowers such as the luscious blooms of lilies (*Lilium*) (3a) borne on tall stems, clumps of little *Dianthus* (3b), and also from herbs like thyme (*Thymus*) and golden marjoram (*Origanum vulgare* 'Aureum') (3c) which have aromatic leaves.

4 Feathery plumes of pink *Astilbe* provide attractive texture and colour.

5 Trailing hardy geraniums (5a) and thyme (5b) soften the brick paving and provide a gentle colour contrast with their pink and mauve flowers.

6 Hardy annuals can be sown in the spaces between permanent plants and will self-sow to give a delightful informal look to the border.

7 Ensure summer-long colour by filling any gaps with frost-tender perennials such as *Argyranthemum* (marguerite).

8 Like these strawberries, edible plants are perfectly at home in the cottage garden border. They will fruit well, given their sunny spot at the front.

the exotic border

4

Create an exotic paradise with huge, dramatic leaves, eye-catching shapes and colours, and a bevy of fabulous flowers in sizzling shades. Few of these flamboyant beauties tolerate frost, but even in cooler areas they can be used to create a stunning seasonal display from midsummer until the first frosts of autumn. Full sun, rich soil and a sheltered site are the vital ingredients for success.

Colour schemes for intense borders are sensational and hot. Reds, oranges and yellows are bright and fiery, with contrasting foliage in purples and rich greens. Use foliage to break up solid blocks of bright flowers or the overall appearance could be overwhelming.

1 Tall, lush foliage is the perfect backdrop to the brilliantly coloured flowers, and green provides a restful contrast to so much vivid colour. Here *Arundo donax* creates a spectacular display of tall bamboo-like stems.

2 *Canna* is invaluable for creating exotic effects, with enormous, paddle-shaped leaves and brightly coloured blooms borne on tall stems. Numerous hybrids offer flowers in many shades of red, orange and yellow, with leaves that are mostly green but in some cases are purple or even striped with different colours.

3 Red *Dahlia* blooms look sultry and theatrical against the purple *Canna* foliage. Compare this to the much lighter and sharper effect that they create in combination with the sparkling yellow French marigolds (4).

4 The smaller-flowered *Tagetes* (French marigolds) lend themselves well to edging and to being used in a mixed planting, with flowers in sunshine shades of yellow and orange.

5 Spiky green leaves make the perfect division between colours, leading the eye upwards for a short distance and encouraging the viewer to pause for a moment. Plants such as *Iris, Sisyrinchium* and *Crocosmia* are ideal for this role.

the gravel border

For a sunny site with well-drained soil all year, choose drought-tolerant plants that come up smiling when the sun bakes down. Cover the ground with gravel to give a crisp, clean finish that sets off plants to perfection. The gravel serves a practical purpose too by keeping plant roots cool and slowing water loss from the soil.

Colour combinations here are fresh and lively, with plenty of blues, yellows and whites as well as vivid shades of pink and orange. With so many bright flowers, foliage and form can be easily overlooked, so include some plants with attractive shapes and leaves to give long-lasting interest and to act as a buffer between the flowers.

1 *Euphorbia characias* subsp. *wulfenii* is invaluable for long-term interest, with acid-green bracts that make a superb contrast of shape as well as colour to the mound of blue *Nepeta* (2).

2 *Nepeta* x *faassenii* is a refreshing colour contrast to the mass of white *Crambe cordifolia* (4). Its lax, spreading shape is particularly good for softening hard edges of paths and borders.

3 *Sedum spectabile* is typical of drought-tolerant plants that have evolved a range of strategies for survival. It has fleshy, succulent leaves to store water. Good for providing foliage interest in spring and summer, it will add lots of colour late in the season with flat heads of bright flowers.

4 *Crambe cordifolia* creates high drama with clouds of small white flowers on tall, branched stems that spring up from basal clumps of huge, dark green leaves.

5 *Verbascum* forms handsome clumps of foliage when young, then shoots up to form 'candles' of colourful flowers in its second year. Silver and grey-leaved plants are a good choice for a gravel garden as nearly all thrive in dry conditions, but take care not to plant too many or the garden could look dull and lifeless on overcast days.

6 *Bergenia* has glossy, rounded leaves that look good all year, and it blooms in late winter to give much needed colour.

the classic border

An informal border with plentiful and exuberant planting is the favourite option for many gardens. A framework of shrubs and evergreens provides all-year structure, often with the bonus of flowers, and this framework is infilled with plants that provide seasonal colour.

Here in midsummer the perennials create a blaze of colour. Bulbs and ornamental grasses could take on this job during spring and autumn.

Colour schemes could be rich and bright – as with this selection of reds, blues and rose-pink – or in soft pastel shades mixed with silver foliage.

1 The fresh green foliage of *Hebe rakaiensis* accentuates the colours of the surrounding flowers. Hebes are excellent structure plants for the middle to front of the border. As well as having evergreen foliage and a bold shape, many produce flowers in summer too.

2 Dark green leaves of *Viburnum tinus* and other shrubs make a handsome backdrop against which to see the range of bright flowers. Though such shrubs are far less exciting than masses of blooms, they really come into their own in winter when there is little else to look at.

3 Spires of *Salvia sylvestris* make a strong combination with the rose-pink *Alstromeria* (4) behind.

4 *Alstromeria* is the eye-catcher in this border, with gleaming pink blooms on tall stems.

5 Neutral shades – here provided by the spiky, silver leaves of *Onopordum* – are invaluable between bright colours.

6 Pretty mauves and blues combine well with most flower and foliage colours. Here *Penstemon heterophyllus* tumbles over the edge of the lawn.

7 Mauves and blues, such as *Nepeta* x *faassenii*, in the background create the illusion of space.

8 Some plants provide their own effective colour contrasts, such as this *Persicaria*, which bears long, tapering, deep red flower spikes against glossy green leaves.

9 Always consider the background colour when choosing flowers. The orange-red blooms of *Lychnis chalcedonica* 'disappear' against the dark brick wall, but picture the difference once the golden-leaved shrub behind has grown sufficiently to create a superb colour contrast.

plant directory

key to symbols

leaf types
- ✍ Deciduous
- ◣ Evergreen

flowering times
- ❶ Spring
- ❷ Summer
- ❸ Autumn
- ❹ Winter

siting
- ○ Full sun
- ◑ Partial shade
- ● Full shade

hardiness
- ❄ Frost–tender
- ❄❄ Grow outside in a sheltered spot
- ❄❄❄ Fully hardy

Abutilon x suntense 'Jermyns'
Shrub

🍃 | ❷ | ○ | ❆ ❆

H 1.8m (6ft) S 1.5m (5ft)
A fast-growing, upright shrub bearing masses of large, blue-mauve, saucer-shaped flowers, and with grey-green toothed leaves. Grow in moderately fertile, well-drained soil.

Acanthus spinosus
Perennial

🍃 | ❶–❷ | ◐ | ❆ ❆ ❆

H 90cm (3ft) S 60cm (2ft)
Bear's breeches have striking tall stems of white flowers with purple bracts rising above a clump of deeply cut, spiny-edged, dark green leaves. Tolerates most soils but prefers one that is deep, fertile and well drained.

Acer palmatum
Shrub

🍃 | ◐ | ❆ ❆ ❆

H 0.9–2.4m (3–8ft) S 0.9–1.5m (3–5ft)
Many varieties of Japanese maple have elegant, deeply cut, red or purple leaves. Plant shape varies from mound-forming 'Dissectum' types to upright ones that grow slowly to small-tree size. The leaf colours are wonderful in autumn. Grow in fertile, moist but well-drained soil, sheltered from cold winds.

Achillea 'Moonshine'
Perennial

🍃 | ❷ | ○ | ❆ ❆ ❆

H 75cm (30in) S 45cm (18in)
This plant has attractive foliage and flowers, with large heads of lemon-yellow flowers borne above fern-like grey-green foliage. Grow in well-drained soil.

Agapanthus
Perennial

🍃 | ❷ | ○ | ❆ ❆

H to 60cm (2ft) S 45cm (18in)
African blue lilies are exotic-looking plants that have stout stems topped with large umbels of bell-shaped flowers, borne above clumps of long, strap-shaped leaves. Most varieties have blue flowers but there are white forms. Grow in a sheltered site in fertile, moist but well-drained soil.

Ajuga reptans 'Burgundy Glow'
Perennial

🍃 | ❶ | ○ ◐ ● | ❆ ❆ ❆

H 15cm (6in) S 60cm (2ft)
This bugle is a good groundcover plant, forming a carpet of oval leaves suffused with deep red and purple tints. In spring it bears spikes of blue flowers. Grow in any reasonably fertile, moisture-retentive soil.

Akebia quinata
Climber

🍃 | ❶ | ○ ◐ | ❆ ❆

H 1.8m (6ft)
A twining climber with attractive blue-green leaves divided into five leaflets, and cup-shaped, purple-red, scented flowers. It needs shelter to protect blooms from late spring frosts. Grow in fertile, moist but well-drained soil.

Alchemilla mollis
Perennial

🍃 | ❷ | ○ ● | ❆ ❆ ❆

H 45cm (18in) S 60cm (2ft)
Lady's mantle has lobed, soft green leaves that are scalloped at the edges and form a spreading mound. It bears stems of lime-yellow flowers. Easy to grow in any reasonable soil.

Allium 'Purple Sensation'
Bulb

🍃 | ❷ | ○ | ❆ ❆ ❆

H 90cm (3ft) S 15cm (6in)
The bold, rounded, deep violet blooms are made up of numerous star-shaped flowers and are borne on tall stems. Grow in fertile, well-drained soil.

Amelanchier lamarckii
Tree

🍃 | ❶ | ○ ◐ | ❆ ❆ ❆

H 3.6m (12ft) S 3m (10ft)
Snowy mespilus is a fast-growing small tree that bears racemes of white flowers, and has attractive rounded leaves and good autumn leaf colour. Grow on fertile, moist but well-drained soil. The best leaf colour occurs when grown on lime-free soil.

Anemone x hybrida 'Queen Charlotte'
Perennial

🍃 | ❷–❸ | ○ ◐ | ❆ ❆ ❆

H to 90cm (3ft) S 60cm (2ft)
The Japanese anemone is a vigorous spreading perennial, sometimes invasive, that produces tall stems topped with many large, saucer-shaped, semi-double, deep pink flowers. Grow in fertile, humus-rich soil that is well drained in winter.

Anthemis punctata subsp. cupaniana
Perennial

🍃 | ❷ | ○ | ❆ ❆

H 30cm (1ft) S 75cm (30in)
This mat-forming perennial has finely divided silver-grey leaves and many small, white, long-lasting, daisy-like flowers. Grow in moderately fertile soil that is very sharply drained.

Anthemis tinctoria
Perennial

🍃 | ❷ | ○ | ❆ ❆ ❆

H to 75cm (30in) S 45cm (18in)
Golden marguerites bear many yellow daisy-like flowers on slender stems above fresh green, fern-like foliage. A.t. 'E.C. Buxton' is lemon-yellow while 'Kelwayi' is bright yellow. Grow on light, well-drained soil.

Aquilegia
Perennial

🍃 | ❷ | ○ ◐ | ❆ ❆ ❆

H to 60cm (2ft) S 30cm (1ft)
Columbines are clump forming with attractively lobed green leaves, from which rise slender stems topped with several bell-shaped flowers. In some varieties the flowers have long spurs. Grow in fertile, preferably moisture-retentive but well-drained soil.

Artemisia 'Powis Castle'
Perennial

🍃 | ❷ | ○ | ❆ ❆ ❆

H 60cm (2ft) S 60cm (2ft)
The very finely divided silvery foliage creates a beautiful effect on a compact, rounded plant. Grow in well-drained soil.

Arum italicum 'Marmoratum'
Perennial

🍃 | ❷ | ○ ● | ❆ ❆ ❆

H 30cm (1ft) S 45cm (18in)
Its large, arrow-shaped leaves are beautifully marbled with pale green and cream; the leaves last from early winter through into spring, followed by spikes of bright orange, toxic berries. Grow in well-drained, humus-rich soil.

Aucuba japonica 'Crotonifolia'
Shrub

🍃 | ❷ | ○ ◐ | ❆ ❆ ❆

H 1.5m (5ft) S 1.2m (4ft)
This spotted laurel's large, glossy leaves are boldly splashed with yellow. Plant out of midday sun as this can cause scorching. Grows in all but very moist soils.

Ballota pseudodictamnus
Shrub

🍃 | ○ | ❆ ❆

H 45cm (18in) S 60cm (2ft)
A mound-forming plant producing woolly stems clothed in rounded, soft-textured, grey-green leaves. Grow in free-draining soil that is low in fertility.

Begonia 'Dragon Wing'
Tuber

🍃 🍃 | ❷ | ○ ◐ | ❆

H 75cm (30in) S 60cm (2ft)
A stunning plant, which forms an upright mound of large, bold leaves heavily flushed with red-purple. It also produces red flowers. Grow in fertile, humus-rich soil in a sheltered site.

Begonia 'Illumination Apricot'
Tuber

🍃 | ❷ | ○ | ❆

H 30cm (1ft) S 75cm (30in)
Excellent in raised containers and hanging baskets, this pendulous variety creates cascades of double orange flowers. Site in sun but out of the hottest midday rays.

Berberis
Shrub

H 1.8m (6ft) S 1.2m (4ft)
Tough and easily grown shrubs. *B. darwinii* forms an upright dome-shaped bush of small, dark green, spiny-toothed leaves, covered with clusters of small dark orange flowers. Grow in any reasonable soil. *B. linearifolia* 'Orange King' has stiffer branches and a more open in habit than *B. darwinii*, this variety also has larger leaves and more substantial flowers.

Beta vulgaris 'Ruby Chard'
Annual/biennial

H and S 60cm (2ft)
Swiss chard is a decorative vegetable with strikingly attractive foliage; the leaves are dark green and the wide midrib bright wine-red – the whole leaf becomes suffused dark red in autumn and winter. Grow in light, fertile, moisture-retentive soil.

Bidens ferulifolia
Perennial

H 15cm (6in) S 90cm (3ft)
A long-flowering trailing plant that bears masses of bright yellow 'daisy' flowers among finely divided green foliage. It is mainly used in containers but is also good for borders. Grow in moist but well-drained soil.

Brunnera macrophylla
Perennial

H and S 60cm (2ft)
Perennial forget-me-nots are clump forming, with heart-shaped green leaves and stems of many small, deep blue flowers. Grow in moderately fertile, moist but well-drained soil.

Calendula officinalis
Annual

H 45cm (18in) S 30cm (2ft)
Pot marigolds are very easily grown hardy annuals that usually self-seed once established, bearing single or double flowers. 'Orange King' and 'Indian Prince' (Prince Series) have bright orange flowers. Best grown on moderately fertile, well-drained soil, but they will tolerate poor soils.

Camellia x williamsii 'Donation'
Shrub

H 1.8m (6ft) S 1.2m (4ft)
This is the most popular of the numerous camellias, and bears semi-double, deep pink blooms that show off beautifully against its glossy, dark green leaves. Grow in moist but well-drained acid soil, in a sheltered site and out of the morning sun.

Canna
Perennial

H to 1.2m (4ft) S 45cm (18in)
Indian shot is an exotic-looking plant with large, brightly coloured flowers borne on tall stems above paddle-shaped leaves. Red varieties include 'Brilliant', 'Endeavour', 'King Humbert' and 'President'. Orange varieties include 'Striata' and 'Wyoming'. Grow in fertile soil and keep well watered.

Chaenomeles
Shrub

H and S 1.8m (6ft)
Flowering quince is a tough and easy shrub that looks best when trained flat against a wall or fence. It bears numerous saucer-shaped blooms along the naked stems in early spring. Grow in any reasonable soil. *C. x superba* 'Crimson & Gold' has bright crimson flowers while those of *C. speciosa* 'Nivalis' are pure white.

Choisya
Shrub

H 1.8m (6ft) S 1.5m (5ft)
The large, lobed leaves of *Choisya ternata*, Mexican orange blossom, are bright green, glossy and light-reflecting. The plant also bears clusters of scented white flowers. Grow in fertile, well-drained soil. *C.t.* 'Sundance' and *C.* 'Goldfingers' have slightly smaller, glossy, bright yellow leaves, which are lobed, deeply so in the case of 'Goldfingers'.

Chrysanthemum segetum
Annual

H 60cm (2ft) S 30cm (1ft)
Also sold as *Xanthophthalum segetum*, corn marigolds are fast-growing, fleshy-leaved hardy annuals, bearing large golden daisy flowers over a long period. Grow on poor to moderately fertile, well-drained soil.

Clematis alpina and C. macropetala varieties
Climbers

H 1.8m (6ft)
These clematis are easy and quick-growing with a wide selection, including many blue-flowered ones. Numerous lantern-shaped, downward facing flowers are borne among divided, fresh green foliage. Grow in fertile, moist but well-drained soil.

Clematis (large-flowered) hybrids
Climbers

H to 3m (10ft)
Noted for their massive, plate-sized flowers, these handsome plants offer a vast selection of different colours. Grow in deep, fertile, moist but well-drained soil, sheltered from winds, with the roots in the shade and top growth in the sun.

Clematis 'Jackmanii'
Climber

H to 3m (10ft) S 1.8m (6ft)
One of the most vigorous and free-flowering of the later-blooming clematis hybrids, bearing masses of large, deep purple blooms. Grow in fertile, humus-rich soil in a sheltered site, with the roots in the shade and top growth in the sun.

Clematis montana
Climber

H 3.6m (12ft)
A fast-growing and very vigorous climber that is smothered in masses of saucer-shaped, pink or white flowers. Some varieties are slightly scented. Grow in fertile, humus-rich soil.

Clematis tangutica
Climber

H 3m (10ft) S 2.4m (8ft)
A long-flowering climber that bears bright yellow lantern-shaped flowers over a long period. The blooms are followed by silky seedheads that are also decorative in appearance. Grow in fertile, humus-rich soil.

Clematis viticella
Climber

H to 2.4m (8ft)
These are fast-growing, adaptable climbers, and more tolerant of adverse conditions than large-flowered hybrids, producing masses of purple blooms for many weeks. 'Etoile Violette' is single while 'Purpurea Plena Elegans' is double and rosette-like. 'Alba Luxurians' bears green-tipped white blooms for many weeks, whereas 'Madame Julia Correvon' has small, wine-red flowers. Grow in fertile, moist but well-drained soil.

Colchicum autumnale 'Pleniflorum'
Bulb

🌱 | ❸ | ○ ◐ ● | ❄ ❄ ❄

H 30cm (1ft) S 45cm (18in)
Meadow saffron is also known as 'naked ladies', because the leaves die back by summer and so the double, lilac-pink blooms appear alone from bare ground. Grow in an open site in fertile, well-drained soil.

Convolvulus cneorum
Shrub

🌿 | ❷ | ○ | ❄ ❄

H and S 45cm (18in)
This is a neat, rounded plant with slender, silky, silver-green leaves. It bears white, funnel-shaped flowers, with yellow centres over a long period. Grow in well-drained soil.

Cordyline australis
Shrub

🌿 | ○ ◐ ● | ❄ ❄

H to 1.5m (5ft) S 90cm (3ft)
The cabbage tree is a palm-like plant with long, slender leaves arching out from the trunk. Several varieties have purple or reddish foliage. Grow in fertile, well-drained soil.

Coreopsis grandiflora
Perennial

🌱 | ❷ | ○ ◐ | ❄ ❄ ❄

H 60cm (2ft) S 45cm (18in)
Often grown as an annual, this plant bears numerous large, bright yellow flowers on slender stems. *C.g.* 'Calypso' has variegated foliage. Grow in fertile, well-drained soil.

Cornus alba
Shrub

🌱 | ○ ◐ | ❄ ❄ ❄

H and S 1.8m (6ft)
C.a. 'Elegantissima' (variegated dogwood) is easy and fast growing, and provides year-round interest with green and white leaves in season and then bright red stems through the winter. The leaves of *C.a.* 'Aurea' (golden dogwood) open bright yellow and become tinged with green by late summer. Again, its red stems provide winter interest. Grow on any but very dry soil.

Cornus controversa 'Variegata'
Shrub

🌱 | ❷ | ○ ◐ | ❄ ❄ ❄

H 1.5m (5ft) S 1.8m (6ft)
The wedding cake tree is a rounded shrub that eventually attains the size of a small tree. Its tiers of branches bear leaves with broad white edges, above which the white flowers are borne in broad, flat clusters. Grow in any reasonably fertile soil.

Cosmos atrosanguineus
Perennial

🌱 | ❷–❸ | ○ | ❄

H 75cm (30in) S 30cm (1ft)
The chocolate plant is a delightful little tender perennial that bears dark red blooms, like those of a miniature dahlia, and it has a rich chocolate scent. Grow in fertile, moist but well-drained soil.

Cosmos bipinnatus
Annual

🌱 | ❷–❸ | ○ | ❄

H to 1.2m (4ft) S 30cm (1ft)
This imposing half-hardy annual bears very large 'daisy' flowers on upright, branching stems which are clothed in feathery green foliage. White varieties include 'Cosmonaut' and 'Purity'. Grow in moderately fertile, moist but well-drained soil.

Cotinus
Shrub

🌱 | ❷ | ○ ◐ | ❄ ❄ ❄

H and S 1.8m (6ft)
The smoke bush is a rounded, bushy shrub with oval leaves that turn a brilliant red in autumn, and plumes of buff or pinkish flowers. Varieties like *C.* 'Grace' and *C. coggygria* 'Royal Purple' are purple-leaved. Grow in fertile, moist but well-drained soil.

Crambe cordifolia
Perennial

🌱 | ❶–❷ | ○ ◐ | ❄ ❄ ❄

H 1.8m (6ft) S 1.2m (4ft)
A substantial perennial, which is spectacular when in flower with its tall, open-branched stems forming a cloud of tiny white blooms. Grow in deep, fertile, well-drained soil.

Crocosmia
Perennial

🌱 | ❷–❸ | ○ ◐ | ❄ ❄ ❄

H 90cm (3ft) S 45cm (18in)
C. x *crocosmiiflora* 'Emily McKenzie' bears clusters of large, downward-facing, vivid orange blooms on tall stems above grass-like foliage. *C.* 'Lucifer' is a stunning late-season perennial with brilliant, clear red blooms on tall stems above long, broad green leaves. These plants look best growing in groups. Grow in moist, fertile, humus-rich soil.

Cyclamen hederifolium
Bulbous perennial

🌱 🌿 | ❸ | ○ ◐ | ❄ ❄ ❄

H 10cm (4in) S 30cm (1ft)
Hardy cyclamens make excellent groundcover under larger plants, their silvery marbled leaves lasting from autumn to late spring. The flowers are deep pink. Grow on humus-rich, well-drained soil.

Cynara cardunculus
Perennial

🌱 | ❷ | ○ | ❄ ❄ ❄

H 1.5m (5ft) S 1.2m (4ft)
The cardoon is an imposing plant that forms a clump of large, divided, silvery leaves, and bears large, blue-purple flowers on tall stems. Grow in fertile, well-drained soil.

Dahlia
Tuber

🌱 | ❷–❸ | ○ | ❄

H to 90cm (3ft) S 45cm (18in)
A number of these eye-catching, late-season plants, such as 'Bednall Beauty' and 'David Howard', have orange flowers. Of the many red dahlias, 'Bishop of Llandaff' is notable for the dark, black-red foliage that makes an outstanding contrast to its clear red, single flowers. Grow in fertile, humus-rich soil and give a liquid feed weekly in summer.

Daphne odora 'Aureomarginata'
Shrub

🌿 | ❶ | ○ | ❄ ❄ ❄

H and S 90cm (3ft)
A rounded evergreen shrub that is renowned for the fragrance of its purple-pink, white-tinged flowers which are borne in small clusters. Grow in moderately fertile, humus-rich but well-drained soil.

Dicentra spectabilis 'Alba'
Perennial

🌱 | ❶ | ○ ◐ | ❄ ❄ ❄

H and S 60cm (2ft)
Bleeding heart's dainty, arching stems are hung with locket-like, pure white flowers, which are more striking than the pink blooms of the species. It can be grown in the sun if the soil is moist. Grow in fertile, humus-rich soil.

Dicksonia antarctica
Fern

🌱 | ❷ | ○ ◐ ● | ❄ ❄

H 1.8m (6ft) S 1.2m (4ft)
This tree fern is a bold architectural plant that produces huge fronds from the top of its fibrous trunk. The trunk must be watered daily during the growing season. Grow on moisture-retentive soil.

Doronicum
Perennial

🌱 | ❶ | ○ ◐ | ❄ ❄ ❄

H and 45cm (18in)
Leopard's bane is an easy clump-forming perennial that bears large, bright yellow flowers above scalloped-edged green leaves. Grow in moist but well-drained soil.

Dryopteris filix-mas
Fern

🌱 | ❷ | ○ or ● | ❄ ❄ ❄

H 1.2m (4ft) S 60cm (2ft)
One of the easiest hardy ferns to grow, the male fern's large leaves rise from the crown to form a bold, upright clump. It prefers moist, humus-rich soil but will tolerate drier conditions.

Eccremocarpus scaber
Climber

🍃 | ❷–❸ | ○ | ❋ ❋

H 2.4m (8ft)
Chilean glory flower is a fast-growing scrambler with clusters of small, tubular, bright orange flowers and grey-green foliage divided into leaflets. Grow in fertile, well-drained soil in a sheltered site.

Elaeagnus x ebbingei
Shrub

🍃 | ❸ | ○ | ❋ ❋ ❋

H 1.8m (6ft) S 1.5m (5ft)
The pointed, leathery leaves of the cultivars are variegated with yellow: 'Gilt Edge' is brighter than 'Limelight'. The flowers are small but strongly scented. Grow in all but very moist soils.

Erica carnea 'Springwood White'
Heather

🍃 | ❹–❺ | ○ ◐ | ❋ ❋ ❋

H 15cm (6in) S to 60cm (2ft)
Winter heath bears masses of tiny, bell-shaped flowers on short stems above a carpet of deep green foliage. Unlike many heathers, this species tolerates mildly alkaline soil and a little shade. Grow in moderately fertile, well-drained soil.

Erysimum
Biennial/perennial

🍃 | ❶ | ○ ◐ | ❋ ❋ ❋

H and S 45cm (18in)
These wallflowers are short lived and usually grown as biennials for spring blooms. E. x allionii and E. cheiri 'Orange Bedder' have glowing orange flowers. Grow on poor to moderately fertile, preferably neutral to alkaline, well-drained soil.

Escallonia 'Iveyi'
Shrub

🍃 | ❷ | ○ | ❋ ❋

H and S 2.4m (8ft)
A rounded shrub, with glossy, deep green leaves, that is smothered in large conical panicles of pure white, scented flowers. Grow in fertile, well-drained soil.

Eschscholzia 'Orange King'
Annual

🍃 | ❷ | ○ | ❋ ❋ ❋

H and S 60cm (2ft)
The Californian poppy bears showy, papery-petalled blooms above feathery foliage; the flowers close in dull weather. Thrives in poor, well-drained soil.

Eucalyptus gunnii
Tree

🍃 | ○ | ❋ ❋ ❋

H 1.8m (6ft) S 1.2m (4ft)
The cider gum will form a tall tree if left unpruned, but for the best foliage prune yearly to maintain a dense, upright shrub with rounded, intensely blue leaves. Grow in well-drained soil.

Eucomis bicolor
Perennial

🍃 | ○ | ❋ ❋

H 60cm (2ft) S 30cm (1ft)
The pineapple flower's wide, bright green, strap-shaped leaves form a semi-upright clump. The numerous tiny, greenish flowers are borne clustered together on upright stems to make an eye-catching display. Grow on fertile, well-drained soil and protect during winter in cold areas.

Euonymus fortunei
Shrub

🍃 | ○ ● | ❋ ❋ ❋

H and S 60–90cm (2–3ft)
A dual-purpose shrub that grows equally well as groundcover or clambering slowly up a wall or fence, 'Silver Queen' has shiny, oval, white-edged green leaves. 'Emerald 'n' Gold' is excellent as groundcover, with small oval leaves that are brightly edged with yellow. Tough and easy to grow on all but very moist soil.

Euonymus japonicus 'Ovatus Aureus'
Shrub

🍃 | ○ ◐ | ❋ ❋ ❋

H 1.2m (4ft) S 60–90cm (2–3ft)
Upright and broadly conical in shape, this shrub has dark green, oval leaves that have wide, yellow edges. It can be trimmed to shape and prefers well-drained soil.

Euphorbia characias 'Silver Swan'
Perennial

🍃 | ○ ◐ | ❋ ❋ ❋

H 90cm (3ft) S 60cm (2ft)
An upright and clump-forming plant that has long, tapered, grey-green leaves broadly edged with creamy white. Grow in moderately fertile, well-drained soil, in a sheltered site.

Euphorbia dulcis 'Chameleon'
Perennial

🍃 | ❶ | ○ ◐ | ❋ ❋ ❋

H and S 60cm (2ft)
This variety of spurge is grown for its attractive foliage and upright stems of decorative bracts. It has rich purple leaves and purple-tinted, yellow-green bracts. It also has good autumn colour. It prefers fertile, moisture-retentive soil but tolerates dry conditions.

Euphorbia griffithii 'Dixter'
Perennial

🍃 | ❷ | ○ ◐ | ❋ ❋ ❋

H and S 75cm (30in)
Striking in both foliage and in the dull orange 'flowers' borne on upright stems with long, dark green leaves, this variety and the similar 'Fireglow' look colourful early in the season. Grow on moist, humus-rich soil.

Euphorbia polychroma
Perennial

🍃 | ❶–❷ | ○ ◐ | ❋ ❋ ❋

H and S 45cm (18in)
A clump-forming plant that bears heads of bright greenish-yellow bracts over a long period. Grows in any reasonable soil that is not too wet.

Exochorda x macrantha 'The Bride'
Shrub

🍃 | ❶ | ○ ◐ | ❋ ❋ ❋

H 1.5m (5ft) S 1.8m (6ft)
Spectacular when in flower, this plant has masses of pure white flowers borne in short racemes against light green foliage. Grow in fertile, moist but well-drained soil.

Fargesia murieliae
Bamboo

🍃 | ○ ● | ❋ ❋ ❋

H to 3m (10ft) S 90cm (3ft)
A handsome, easily grown bamboo that forms an upright to slightly arching clump of canes topped with lance-shaped, green leaves. Grow in fertile, moisture retentive soil.

Fatsia japonica
Shrub

🍃 | ○ ● | ❋ ❋

H and S 1.8m (6ft)
Huge, glossy, light-reflecting leaves and an attractive shape make the Japanese aralia an immensely useful shrub. Grow in fertile, moist but well-drained soil.

Felicia amelloides
Sub-shrub

🍃 | ❷ | ○ | ❋

H and S 45cm (18in)
Blue marguerites are compact, rounded plants mostly used in summer containers. The small, sky-blue flowers are borne on slender stems and have contrasting yellow centres. Grow in moderately fertile, well-drained soil.

Festuca glauca
Grass

🍃 | ❷ | ○ | ❋ ❋ ❋

H and S 45cm (18in)
Blue fescue is a densely growing grass that forms a neat clump of intensely blue leaves and produces spikelets of blue-green flowers. Grow in well-drained soil.

Foeniculum vulgare 'Purpureum'
Perennial

🍃 | ❷ | ○ ◐ | ❋ ❋ ❋

H 1.2m (4ft) S 60cm (sft)
Bronze fennel has a basal clump of feathery, purple-tinged, green leaves. The tall stems are sparsely clad with foliage and topped with flat heads made up of numerous tiny yellow flowers. It self-seeds freely and prefers well-drained soil.

Forsythia
Shrub
✿ | ❶ | ○◔ | ❈❈❈

H 2.4m (8ft) S 1.8m (6ft)
A fast-growing shrub that is smothered in bright yellow flowers in spring, but has little to recommend it for the rest of the year. *F. suspensa* can be trained against a wall or fence. Grows in any reasonable soil.

Fremontodendron 'California Glory'
Shrub
✿🍃 | ❷ | ○ | ❈❈

H and S 3m (10ft)
Huge, waxy-petalled, golden yellow flowers make a spectacular display. Train it against a sheltered wall or fence in all but mild areas. Grow in poor to moderately fertile, preferably neutral to alkaline, well-drained soil.

Fuchsia 'Mrs Popple'
Shrub
✿ | ❷–❸ | ○◔ | ❈❈

H and S 75cm (30in)
Long-flowering and easy to grow in a sheltered spot, this fuchsia makes an excellent display of red-scarlet flowers with purple centres. Prefers fertile, moist but well-drained soil.

Geranium phaeum
Perennial
✿🍃 | ❷ | ◑ or ● | ❈❈❈

H and S 60cm (2ft)
Stems of small, deep purple flowers, with reflexed petals, are borne on short stems above a mound of soft green, deeply lobed leaves. Grow in moderately fertile, moist but well-drained soil.

Geranium psilostemon
Perennial
✿🍃 | ❷ | ○ | ❈❈❈

H 1.2m (4ft) S 75cm (30in)
Bold and dramatic, this geranium (or Armenian cranesbill) forms a lovely display of brilliant magenta, black-centred flowers. Grow in moderately fertile, well-drained soil.

Geranium renardii
Perennial
✿🍃 | ❷ | ○ | ❈❈❈

H and S 30cm (1ft)
Compact and clump-forming, this species is grown more for its attractively puckered sage-green leaves than its white to mauve-flushed flowers. Grow in fertile, well-drained soil.

Geranium 'Rozanne'
Perennial
✿🍃 | ❷ | ○◔ | ❈❈❈

H 30cm (1ft) S 60cm (2ft)
While a number of hardy geraniums have attractive blue flowers, those of 'Rozanne' are outstanding – large, violet blue, with a light blue centre – and borne on spreading plants. Grow on fertile, moist but well-drained soil.

Gleditsia triacanthos 'Sunburst'
Tree
✿🍃 | ○ | ❈❈❈

H to 10m (33ft) S to 8m (26ft)
The honey locust is broadly conical with fern-like, golden yellow leaves that open in late spring, and turn light green by late summer and gold in autumn. Prefers well drained soil.

Gypsophila paniculata 'Bristol Fairy'
Perennial
✿🍃 | ❷ | ○ | ❈❈

H and S 90cm (3ft)
Baby's breath bears numerous small, double, pure white flowers on tall, open-branched stems to appear as a cloud of blossom. Grow in deep, moderately fertile, well-drained soil.

Hakonechloa macra 'Aureola'
Grass
✿🍃 | ○◑ | ❈❈❈

H 45cm (18in) S 60cm (2ft)
Japanese golden grass forms a clump of arching leaves, which are bright yellow striped narrowly with green. Prefers fertile, well drained soil.

Hebe
Shrub
✿🍃 | ❷ | ○ | ❈❈

H and S 30–90cm (2–3ft)
Of this large and useful group of shrubs, varieties such as H. 'Clear Skies', *H. pimeloides* 'Quicksilver' and *H. pinguifolia* 'Pagei' have silver-grey or blue-grey foliage. These varieties have white or mauve flowers. Grow in well-drained soil.

Helichrysum petiolare
Shrub
✿🍃 | ❷ | ○ | ❈

H 45cm (18in) S 60cm (2ft)
This mound-forming to spreading shrub with rounded grey leaves produces heads of white flowers. It is usually used for summer pots and bedding. Grow in well-drained, neutral to alkaline soil.

Heliopsis 'Loraine Sunshine'
Perennial
✿🍃 | ❷ | ○ | ❈❈❈

H 90cm (3ft) S 45cm (18in)
While there are many attractive yellow ox-eyes with large daisy-like flowers, this variety is particularly attractive because of its accompanying green-and-white variegated foliage. Grow in moderately fertile, moist but well-drained soil.

Helleborus
Perennial
✿🍃 | ❶ | ○◔ | ❈❈❈

H and S 60–90cm (2–3ft)
H. argutifolius (Corsican hellebore) has attractive foliage and flowers, with leathery, divided, dark green leaves and clusters of many small, apple-green flowers. Grow in any neutral to alkaline soil. Although less architectural than *H. argutifolius*, *H. foetidus* (stinking hellebore) is excellent for shady spots with its narrow, dark green leaves and large clusters of pale green flowers.

Heuchera
Perennial
✿🍃 | ❷ | ○◔ | ❈❈❈

H and S to 45cm (18in)
A neat, clump-forming perennial, with decorative lobed leaves, that is excellent for edging and groundcover. It bears wiry stems of small, white or pink flowers and many varieties have purple or red leaves. Grow in fertile, moist but well-drained, neutral soil.

Hibiscus syracius 'Oiseau Bleu'
Shrub
✿🍃 | ❷–❸ | ○ | ❈❈❈

H 1.5m (5ft) S 1.2m (4ft)
A useful late-flowering shrub that bears many large, open, saucer-shaped, bright blue flowers. It flowers freely only in areas with long, hot summers. Grow in moist but well-drained, neutral to alkaline soil.

Hosta
Perennial
✿🍃 | ❷ | ◑ or ● | ❈❈❈

H and S 30–90cm (1–3ft)
H. 'Big Daddy' and 'Halcyon' are among the few blue-grey plants that thrive in shade. The former bears white flowers and the latter lavender ones on tall stems. Numerous varieties of this lush, large-leaved perennial have variegated leaves, as well as flowers on tall stems. Popular varieties include 'Francee', 'Ground Master' and *H. fortunei* var. *albopicta*. Grow in moisture-retentive soil in borders or containers.

Humulus lupulus 'Aureus'
Climber
✿🍃 | ○◑ | ❈❈❈

H 4m (13ft)
Golden hop is a fast-growing, twining climber with large, lobed, golden leaves. It dies back completely to ground level in winter and prefers reasonably well-drained soil.

Hyacinthus
Bulb

🌿 | ◐ | ○◑ | ❄ ❄

H 30cm (1ft) S 20cm (8in)
Immensely popular for their fragrance, hyacinths form large, upright heads of flowers in many colours including white, blue, pink and red. Grow in any moderately fertile, well-drained soil and protect container-grown bulbs from excessive winter cold and wet.

Hydrangea macrophylla 'Mariesii Perfecta'
Shrub

🌿 | ❷ | ◑ or ● | ❄ ❄ ❄

H and S 1.2m (4ft)
One of the most handsome 'lacecap' hydrangeas, it bears large, flattened heads of rich blue to lilac-mauve flowers. Grow in humus-rich, moderately fertile, moist but well-drained acid soil, and shelter it from cold winds.

Hydrangea paniculata 'Grandiflora'
Shrub

🌿 | ❷–❸ | ○◑ | ❄ ❄ ❄

H and S 1.8m (6ft)
Spectacular when in flower, this variety bears so many large, conical heads of creamy-white flowers that the stems arch under their weight. Grow in moderately fertile, moist but well-drained soil.

Hypericum 'Hidcote'
Shrub

🌿 | ❷–❸ | ○◑ | ❄ ❄ ❄

H and S 1.2m (4ft)
Tough and easy to grow, this rounded bush bears large, saucer-shaped, golden-yellow flowers. Grow in any reasonable soil that is not too wet or dry.

Iberis sempervirens 'Schneeflocke'
Subshrub

🌿 | ◐ | ○ | ❄ ❄ ❄

H 25cm (10in) S 60cm (2ft)
Candytuft shows off its masses of rounded heads of pure white flowers against its dark green foliage. Grow on poor to moderately fertile, moist but well-drained, neutral to alkaline soil.

Ilex
Shrub/tree

🌿 | ○◑ | ❄ ❄ ❄

H 1.5m (5ft) S 90cm (3ft)
Relatively slow-growing but useful, holly responds well to shaping and trimming and so can be used as a specimen, a hedge or left to grow as a small tree. The best variegated ones include *I. aquifolium* 'Argentea Marginata', *I.a.* 'Ferox Argentea' and *I.a.* 'Silver Queen'. *I. altaclerensis* 'Golden King' has glossy, spiny leaves that are brightly variegated green and gold. They prefer fertile, moist but well-drained soil.

Ipomoea tricolor 'Heavenly Blue'
Annual climber

🌿 | ❷ | ○ | ❄

H 1.8m (6ft)
Morning glory is a fast grower that bears large, saucer-shaped flowers, which are deep sky-blue with a white eye. Each bloom lasts for less than a day, but the flowers are produced in great profusion. Grow in fertile, moist but well-drained soil in a warm sheltered site.

Iris foetidissima
Perennial

🌿 | ❷ | ○ ● | ❄ ❄ ❄

H 60cm (2ft) S 45cm (18in)
The pale yellow flowers of the Gladwyn iris are less notable than its glossy evergreen foliage and swollen seed pods that split to reveal bright orange seeds. It grows in any reasonable soil and tolerates dry conditions.

Iris pallida 'Argentea Variegata'
Perennial

🌿 | ❷ | ○ | ❄ ❄ ❄

H 60cm (2ft) S 30cm (1ft)
This small but striking, clump-forming plant has attractive grey-green and white-striped leaves, and large, pale blue flowers that are borne on short stems. Grow in fertile, well-drained, neutral to acid soil.

Iris sibirica
Perennial

🌿 | ❷ | ○◑ | ❄ ❄ ❄

H 60cm (2ft) S 30cm (1ft)
The upright stems of the Siberian iris are topped with several attractively marked blooms, borne well above the clumps of grass-like foliage. Numerous cultivars are available in a range of colours, although blues remain the most popular. Grow in well-drained, moderately fertile, neutral to acid soil.

Jasminum officinale
Climber

🌿 | ❷ | ○◑ | ❄ ❄

H and S 2.4–3m (8–10ft)
In addition to the green-leaved species, two varieties have decorative foliage: *J.o.* 'Argenteovariegata' (summer jasmine) is a twining climber with attractive, pinnate, grey-green leaves that are boldly edged with creamy white. It bears clusters of fragrant white flowers. Grow in fertile, moist but well-drained soil. *J.o.* 'Fiona Sunrise' has attractively shaped bright gold leaves and bears clusters of scented, white flowers. Grows in all but very dry or wet soils.

Juniperus
Conifer

🌿 | ○ | ❄ ❄ ❄

H 30cm (1ft) S to 1.5m (5ft)
J. horizontalis 'Glauca' and *J. squamata* 'Blue Carpet' form ground-hugging carpets of branches clothed with intense silver-blue, needle-like leaves. Grow in well-drained soil.

Kerria japonica 'Pleniflora'
Shrub

🌿 | ◐ | ○ ● | ❄ ❄ ❄

H 2.4m (8ft) S 1.8m (6ft)
Masses of pompom-like, double, bright orange-yellow blooms are borne on arching branches. Although it is deciduous, the light green stems provide winter interest. Grow on any reasonably fertile soil.

Lavandula angustifolia
Shrub

🌿 | ❷ | ○ ● | ❄ ❄ ❄

H and S 45cm (18in)
Lavender is a popular shrub with fragrant blue flowers borne on slender stems, and aromatic, grey-green foliage. Good varieties of the many available are 'Hidcote', 'Munstead' and 'Twickel Purple'. Grow in moderately fertile, well-drained soil.

Lavatera olbia
Shrub

🌿 | ❷–❸ | ○ | ❄ ❄ ❄

H 2.4m (8ft) S 1.8m (6ft)
A fast-growing and extremely long-flowering shrub that bears numerous large, saucer-shaped flowers for months. Tree mallow's colours range from white and pale pink through to rich, dark pink. Grow on light, well-drained soil in a site sheltered from strong winds.

Leycesteria formosa
Shrub

🌿 | ❷ | ○◑ | ❄ ❄

H 1.8m (6ft) S 1.5m (5ft)
Himalayan honeysuckle is a fast grower that bears dangling racemes of white flowers with prominent purple bracts, followed by claret-coloured berries. Green stems look good in winter. Grow in moderate fertile, well-drained soil.

Ligustrum ovalifolium 'Aureum'
Shrub

🌿 | ○◑ | ❄ ❄ ❄

H and S to 3m (10ft)
Golden privet's oval leaves are rich green with wide, bright yellow edges. It responds to trimming and grows in any reasonably well-drained soil.

Lilium
Bulb
🌿 | ❷ | ○ | ❄❄❄
H to 90cm (3ft) S 30cm (1ft)
White predominates among these spectacular flowering plants. Popular examples include *L. longiflorum*, *L.* 'Casa Blanca', *L.* 'Kyoto' and *L. regale*. Several outstanding orange varieties including *L.* 'Enchantment', *L.* 'Fire King' and *L.* 'Jetfire'. These lilies all ideal for containers as well as borders. Grow in a fertile, humus-rich soil or loam-based potting compost, with the roots in the shade.

Liriope muscari
Perennial
🌿 | ❸ | ○◑ | ❄❄❄
H and S 30cm (1ft)
Small spikes of rich, violet-purple flowers make lilyturf useful for late-season colour, and the neat clumps of grass-like foliage provide good all-year interest. Grow in light, moderately fertile soil, sheltered from winds.

Lonicera nitida 'Baggesen's Gold'
Shrub
🌿 | ○● | ❄❄❄
H 1.5m (5ft) S 1.2m (4ft)
The tiny leaves are bright yellow in the sun and lime-green in shade. Responds well to trimming. Grow in all but very moist soil.

Lunaria annua
Biennial
🌿 | ❶ | ○◑ | ❄❄❄
H 60cm (2ft) S 30cm (1ft)
Honesty's upright stems with many small, pale to deep purple flowers rise from a clump of heart-shaped, toothed, green leaves. The flowers are followed in autumn by flat, silvery seed pods. *L.a.* var. *albiflora* has white flowers. They prefer fertile, moist but well-drained soil but will tolerate poorer soils.

Lychnis chalcedonica
Perennial
🌿 | ❷ | ○◑ | ❄❄❄
H 90cm (3ft) S 45cm (18in)
The attractive, clear, orange-red blooms of Maltese cross are borne on upright stems. The large, flat heads are made up of many small, star-shaped flowers. Grow in well-drained soil.

Lychnis coronaria 'Alba'
Perennial
🌿 | ❷ | ○ | ❄❄❄
H 75cm (30in) S 45cm (18in)
Dusty miller's upright, branched stems are clothed in woolly, silver-grey leaves and bear many open, rounded, pure white flowers. Grow in moderately fertile, well-drained soil.

Lysimachia nummularia 'Aurea'
Perennial
🌿 | ❷ | ○● | ❄❄❄
H 10cm (4in) S 60cm (2ft)
Golden creeping Jenny is a useful groundcover and container plant, which forms a carpet of oval golden leaves and bears golden flowers. Grow on all but dry soils.

Mahonia x media
Shrub
🌿 | ❹–❶ | ○● | ❄❄❄
H to 1.8m (6ft) S 1.2m (4ft)
This plant's bold, pinnate, dark green leaves and bright yellow, sweetly-scented flowers make it valuable for winter. Grow in moderately fertile, moist but well-drained soil.

Malus 'Royal Beauty'
Tree
🌿 | ❶ | ○ | ❄❄❄
H 1.8m (6ft) S 1.5m (5ft)
This compact weeping crab apple has large, rounded, reddish-purple leaves that eventually turn dark green. Red-purple flowers are followed in autumn by dark red fruits. Grow in fertile, moist but well-drained soil.

Meconopsis cambrica
Perennial
🌿 | ❶–❷ | ○● | ❄❄❄
H 45cm (18in) S 30cm (1ft)
The Welsh poppy bears papery-petalled, lemon-yellow flowers on slender stems above clumps of light green leaves. It is easy to grow in any reasonably well-drained soil, and self-seeds readily.

Melianthus major
Shrub
🌿 | ❷ | ○ | ❄
H to 1.8m (6ft) S 1.2m (4ft)
The honey bush is an immensely attractive and striking shrub with grey-green to blue-grey leaves that are divided into toothed leaflets. It also bears clusters of scented, brownish-red flowers. Grow in fertile, well-drained soil.

Mimulus aurantiacus
Shrub
🌿 | ❷–❸ | ○ | ❄
H and S 60cm (2ft)
This lax, open shrub has numerous orange flowers that are shown off against small, dark green, sticky leaves. Grow in well-drained, moderately fertile soil and in a sheltered site.

Monarda 'Cambridge Scarlet'
Perennial
🌿 | ❷–❸ | ○ | ❄❄❄
H 75cm (30in) S 60cm (2ft)
Strikingly handsome when it is in bloom, bergamot's tubular, dark red flowers are produced in large whorls on top of tall stems and are very attractive to bees. Grow in any reasonable soil.

Musa basjoo
Perennial
🌿 | ❷ | ○ | ❄❄❄
H to 1.8m (6ft) S to 1.2m (4ft)
The Japanese banana has glossy, bright green leaves. These are narrow and up to 1m (about 3ft) long, and arch out from the stem to make a striking and substantial plant. It sometimes produces pale yellow flowers. Grow in fertile, humus-rich soil.

Muscari armeniacum
Bulb
🌿 | ❶ | ○◑ | ❄❄❄
H 20cm (8in) S 15cm (6in)
The 'cones' of deep blue flowers are borne on short stems above grassy foliage. Grape hyacinths often self-seed to form larger clumps that are good for underplanting shrubs and roses. Grow in moderately fertile, moist but well-drained soil.

Myosotis sylvatica
Biennial
🌿 | ❶ | ○◑ | ❄❄❄
H and S 20cm (8in)
Easy and free flowering, the popular forget-me-not is invaluable for spring bedding, forming carpets of blue flowers. It self-seeds readily.

Narcissus
Bulb
🌿 | ❶ | ○◑ | ❄❄❄
H to 60cm (2ft)
Daffodils are hugely popular spring flowers, offering a wealth of yellow varieties, many of which are scented. Cluster-flowered varieties such as 'Quail' are among the longest-flowering. Grow on any reasonable soil that is not too wet or too dry.

Nepeta x faasenii
Perennial
🌿 | ❷–❸ | ○ | ❄❄❄
H and S 60cm (2ft)
Catmint forms a low, spreading clump of long stems clothed with toothed, aromatic, grey-green leaves and bears masses of blue-mauve flowers over a long period. As its common name suggests, it is attractive to cats. Grow in moderately fertile, well-drained soil.

Nicotiana sylvestris
Annual/perennial
🌿 | ❷–❸ | ○ | ❄
H 1.5m (5ft) S 60cm (2ft)
The tobacco plant is a perennial, but is usually grown as an annual in cold areas. Its tall stems are topped with long-tubed, trumpet-shaped white flowers, above large, paddle-shaped, fresh green leaves. Grow in fertile, moist but well-drained soil.

Nigella damascana
Annual
🍃 | ❷ | ○ | ✳ ✳ ✳
H 45cm (18in) S 10cm (4in)
Love-in-a-mist is an easy-to-grow, hardy annual with attractive flowers, foliage and seedheads. Deep blue flowers, with a surrounding 'ruff' of foliage, are borne on upright stems. Grows on any well-drained soil and self-seeds freely.

Onopordum nervosum
Biennial
🍃 | ❷ | ○ | ✳ ✳ ✳
H to 2.4m (8ft) S 60cm (2ft)
The Scotch thistle is a short lived but imposing architectural plant. It forms a rosette of spiny silver leaves, from which rises a tall stem topped with purple-pink flowers. Grow in well-drained, neutral to alkaline soil.

Ophiopogon planiscapus 'Nigrescens'
Perennial
🍃 | ❷ | ○ ◑ | ✳ ✳ ✳
H and S 30cm (1ft)
Grass-like in appearance, this lilyturf forms a neat, rounded clump. Its curving, strap-shaped leaves are almost black and small sprays of tiny white flowers are followed by black berries. Grow in fertile, moist but well-drained soil.

Papaver orientale
Perennial
🍃 | ❶–❷ | ○ ◑ | ✳ ✳ ✳
H and S to 75cm (30in)
The massive flowers of Oriental poppies are most striking in their red forms like 'Allegro' and 'Beauty of Livermere', which show off against the jagged, green leaves. Grow in deep, fertile, well-drained soil.

Papaver rhoeas
Annual
🍃 | ❷ | ○ | ✳ ✳ ✳
H 60–90cm (2–3ft) S 30cm (1ft)
The field poppy is easy to grow and ideal for a wild or meadow garden, with scarlet flowers borne on long, slender stems. It self-seeds freely and tolerates any well-drained soil.

Passiflora caerulea
Climber
🍃 | ❷–❸ | ○ ◑ | ✳ ✳
H to 3m (10ft)
The blue passion flower is a fast-growing climber with blue and white, bowl-shaped flowers that show well against its lobed, dark green foliage. 'Constance Elliott' has fragrant white flowers with pale blue or white filaments. Grow in moderately fertile, moist but well-drained soil.

Pelargonium
Perennial
🍃 | ❷–❸ | ○ | ✳
H to 45cm (18in) S 30cm (1ft)
Also called geraniums, these are outstanding for long-flowering displays in pots and borders. Red is the classic colour, and is offered by many different varieties. Grow in fertile, well-drained soil in a sheltered spot.

Penstemon 'Garnet'
Perennial
🍃 | ❷–❸ | ○ | ✳ ✳
H and S 60cm (2ft)
Sometimes sold as P. 'Andenken an Friedrich Hahn', this is supremely long-flowering, with funnel-shaped, deep wine-red flowers that are borne above a rounded bush of fresh green foliage. Grow in very well-drained soil, which is preferably not too fertile.

Penstemon heterophyllus
Subshrub
🍃 | ❷–❸ | ○ | ✳ ✳
H 45cm (18in) S 60cm (2ft)
This plant produces racemes of blue-mauve, tubular flowers over a long period. Grow in well-drained, poor to moderately fertile soil.

Persicaria microcephala 'Red Dragon'
Perennial
🍃 | ❷ | ○ ◑ | ✳ ✳
H to 60cm (2ft) S 45cm (18in)
The large, pointed leaves are unusual colours – mostly purple to maroon with burgundy centres, surrounded by a white to pale green chevron and are borne on bright red stems.

Philadelphus
Shrub
🍃 | ❷ | ○ ◑ | ✳ ✳ ✳
H to 2.4m (8ft) S to 1.5m (5ft)
The mock orange bears masses of saucer-shaped, fragrant, white flowers strong fragrance. Varieties differ in size from the compact 'Manteau d'Hermine' at 1m (about 3ft) to the much more vigorous 'Virginal'. Grow in any reasonably fertile, well-drained soil.

Phormium
Shrub
🍃 | ❷ | ○ | ✳ ✳
H 1.2m (4ft) S 90cm (3ft)
New Zealand flax forms an upright clump of long, broad, sword-shaped leaves. A number of varieties have foliage that is partly or fully coloured with red or purple. The flowers are produced on tall stems. Grow in fertile, moist but well-drained soil. Give winter protection in cold areas.

Phygelius aequalis 'Yellow Trumpet'
Shrub
🍃 | ❷–❸ | ○ | ✳ ✳
H 1.2m (4ft) S 90cm (3ft)
An exotic-looking plant that bears many tubular, pale yellow flowers on upright stems above pale green foliage. Grow in fertile, moist but well-drained soil.

Physocarpus opulifolius
Shrub
🍃 | ○ ◑ | ✳ ✳ ✳
H and S 1.8m (6ft)
P.o. 'Diabolo' is a rounded, suckering shrub with lobed, dark purple leaves, and bears small, white to pink-tinged flowers. P.o. 'Dart's Gold' has leaves that open bright yellow and age to greeny-gold. Grow in fertile, moist but well-drained soil, preferably acid.

Pleioblastus auricomus
Bamboo
🍃 | ○ ◑ | ✳ ✳ ✳
H 45cm (18in) S 60cm (2ft)
A neat dwarf bamboo that forms a small clump of green-and-gold striped leaves. Thrives in all but very dry or very wet soil.

Potentilla fruticosa
Shrub
🍃 | ❷–❸ | ○ ◑ | ✳ ✳ ✳
H and S to 1.2m (4ft)
Many varieties of this shrub bear yellow flowers, such as 'Elizabeth', 'Goldfinger' and 'Katherine Dykes'. 'Tangerine' is a long-flowering shrub that bears numerous small, saucer-shaped, orange flowers against divided, fern-like foliage. 'Red Ace' has red-orange flowers and reaches 75cm (30in). Grow in any moderately fertile, well-drained soil.

Primula veris
Perennial
🍃 | ❶ | ○ ◑ | ✳ ✳ ✳
H 20cm (8in) S 15cm (6in)
Cowslips are small, clump-forming plants that bear many heads of golden-yellow, fragrant flowers. Grow in any moderately fertile soil, preferably moist but well-drained.

Prunus avium 'Plena'
Tree
🍃 | ❶ | ○ ◑ | ✳ ✳ ✳
H 4.5m (15ft) S 3m (10ft)
A spreading, dome-shaped tree, the double wild cherry is smothered with clusters of bowl-shaped, white flowers. The red bark provides some winter interest. Grow in moist but well-drained, moderately fertile soil.

Prunus incisa 'Kojo-no-mai'
Shrub
🍃 | ❶ ❷ | ○ | ✳ ✳ ✳
H 90cm (3ft) S 60cm (2ft)
The name translates as 'flight of butterflies', which is very apt when the delicately contorted branches are wreathed in pink flowers. Grow in moist but well-drained, moderately fertile soil.

Prunus lusitanica
Shrub
🍃 | ❷ | ○ ● | ✳ ✳ ✳
H to 3m (10ft) S to 2m (7ft)
Portuguese laurel is useful for year-round structure. It has oval, dark green leaves and responds well to trimming. White flowers are borne on unpruned plants. Grow on all but very wet or dry soils.

plant directory 139

Pulmonaria
Perennial

🌿| ❶ ❷ |○● | ✳✳✳

H 30cm (1ft) S 45cm (18in)
One of the earliest perennials to bloom, lungwort bears clusters of funnel-shaped flowers on short stems above a spreading clump of foliage. Most varieties are blue but there are also pink and white forms. Grow in fertile, moisture-retentive but well-drained soil.

Pyracantha 'Saphyr Orange'
Shrub

🌿| ❶ |○● | ✳✳✳

H and S 2.4m (8ft)
Large clusters of glowing orange autumn berries are the main feature of this firethorn, although its white flowers do provide spring interest. It grows best when trained against a wall, fence or other support. This variety is resistant to the scab disease that troubles many others. Grow in fertile, well-drained soil.

Rhamnus alaternus 'Argenteovariegata'
Shrub

🌿| ❷ |○ | ✳✳✳

H 1.8m (6ft) S 1.5m (5ft)
Italian buckthorn is a fast-growing, broadly conical shrub with oval, grey-green leaves with bold white margins. It also bears clusters of yellow-green flowers and responds well to trimming and shaping. Grow in moderately fertile, well-drained soil.

Rhododendron
Shrub

🌿| ❶ |○◑ | ✳✳✳

H to 1.8cm (6ft) S 1.5cm (5ft)
These glossy-leaved, evergreen shrubs are renowned for their superb displays of brightly coloured spring flowers. Numerous varieties offer an enormous choice of colours and sizes. Grow in acid, moist but well-drained, humus-rich soil.

Ribes speciosum
Shrub

🌿| ❶–❷ |○ | ✳✳✳*

H 1.2m (4ft) S 90cm (3ft)
The flowering currant's dark red flowers hang from the upright branches among the lobed, fresh green leaves, rather like the blooms of a fuchsia. Grow in moderately fertile, well-drained soil.

Rosa
Rose

🌿| ❷–❸ |○ | ✳✳✳

H variable S variable
Roses offer a wide selection of red-flowering varieties such as 'Flower Carpet Red Velvet' and 'Hampshire' (groundcover), 'Climbing Etiole de Hollande' and 'Dublin Bay', (climber), 'Alexander' (hybrid tea) and 'Eye Paint' (floribunda). Numerous roses of all types offer yellow flowers in shades from pale creamy yellow to deep gold. Popular ones include 'Golden Showers' (climber), 'Laura Ford' (miniature climber), 'Graham Thomas' (shrub), 'Grandpa Dickson' (hybrid tea), 'Korresia' (floribunda) and 'Norfolk' (groundcover). Varieties with rich, velvety, purple blooms include 'Cardinal de Richelieu', 'The Prince', 'Tuscany Superb' and 'William Shakespeare 2000'. The flowers of 'Ferdinand Pichard' are purple-striped. White-flowered varieties include 'Climbing Iceberg' (climber), 'Mme Hardy' (shrub), 'Rambling Rector' (rambler), 'Flower Carpet White' (groundcover) and 'Winchester Cathedral' (shrub). Grow in fertile, humus-rich soil.

Ruta graveolens 'Jackman's Blue'
Shrub

🌿| ❷ |○◑ | ✳✳✳

H and S 60cm (2ft)
This rue is rounded, with deeply divided, intense blue-green leaves that have a strong, pungent smell when bruised and clusters of insignificant yellow flowers. Grow in well-drained soil. Important: contact with the foliage may cause severe skin rashes.

Salix exigua
Shrub

🌿|○◑ | ✳✳✳

H and S to 3m (10ft)
Coyote willow is a graceful, upright shrub that bears long, slender, grey-green leaves, which are more silvery when young. Grows on all except dry soils.

Salvia patens
Perennial

🌿| ❷–❸ |○◑ | ✳

H 60cm (2ft) S 45cm (18in)
Grown as an annual in cold areas, this plant bears open-mouthed flowers in a beautiful and unusual shade of clear deep blue on upright stems. Grow on light, moderately fertile, moist but well-drained soil.

Sambucus nigra 'Black Beauty'
Shrub

🌿| ❶ |○◑ | ✳✳✳

H and S 2.4m (8ft)
Purple elder is a fast-growing and easy shrub that creates an attractive combination of flowers and foliage, with large purple leaves and heads of pink flowers. Grows in most soils but does best in fertile, moist but well-drained soil.

Sambucus racemosa 'Plumosa Aurea'
Shrub

🌿|○◑ | ✳✳✳

H and S 2.4m (8ft)
Golden elder is an easy and fast-growing shrub with divided leaves, which are rich gold when young. Prune in spring to encourage plenty of bright foliage. Grows in any reasonable soil.

Santolina pinnata subsp. neapolitana
Shrub

🌿| ❷ |○ | ✳✳✳

H and S 60cm (2ft)
The most attractive of the silvery santolinas, this species has finely divided, silvery foliage and button-like yellow flowerheads. Grow in well-drained soil that is low in fertility.

Santolina rosmarinifolia
Shrub

🌿| ❷ |○ | ✳✳✳

H 60cm (2ft) S 90cm (3ft)
The vivid green, finely cut leaves of this compact shrub can be kept neatly trimmed to form low hedging. It bears button-like, yellow flowers. Grow on well-drained soil.

Sarcococca
Shrub

🌿| ❹ |○● | ✳✳✳

H 60cm (2ft) S to 90cm (3ft)
Sweet box is a small, compact, clump-forming shrub with upright stems that are clothed with pointed, glossy, dark green leaves. It bears many 'tassels' of creamy white, strongly scented flowers. Grow in moist but well-drained, moderately fertile soil.

Saxifraga 'Black Ruby'
Perennial

🌿| ❸ |○● | ✳✳✳

H and S 60cm (2ft)
This is a compact, clump-forming perennial with scalloped-edged, dark reddish-purple leaves. The slender, upright stems of many tiny, white flowers create a handsome contrast. Grow in moist, well-drained, humus-rich soil.

Schizostylis coccinea 'Major'
Perennial

🌿| ❸–❹ |○◑ | ✳✳

H 60cm (2ft) S 30cm (1ft)
The kaffir lily is very late-flowering, often extending into winter in favourable weather, with large red blooms borne on stiff stems and with broad grass-like foliage. Keep it well watered for a good show of flowers. Prefers reasonably fertile, moisture-retentive soil.

Scilla sibirica
Bulb

🌿| ❶ |○◑ | ✳✳✳

H and S 10cm (4ft)
The Siberian squill bears dainty little flowers of an intense shade of bright blue on short stems early in the season. Grow on humus-rich, fertile, well-drained soil.

Sedum
Perennial
🌿 | ❷-❸ | ○ | ✳✳✳
H 60cm (2ft) S 45cm (18in)
S. 'Purple Emperor' has large, flat heads made up of numerous tiny, purple flowers which are borne over a long period. It is a rounded, clump-forming plant with fleshy, purple-tinged leaves. 'Autumn Joy' (also sold as *S. Herbstfreude*) flowers open deep pink and age to copper-red and are popular with bees. 'Ruby Glow' is similar, but the flowers are rust-red. Grow in moderately fertile, well-drained soil.

Senecio cinerea 'Silver Dust'
Shrub
🌿 | ❷ | ○ | ✳✳
H and S 30cm (1ft)
This plant is often grown as an annual, because the deeply divided, white-grey leaves make an excellent foil to the brightly coloured flowers of other plants. Its own yellow flowers are borne from the second year onwards. Grow in well-drained soil.

Sisyrinchium striatum 'Aunt May'
Perennial
🌿 | ❷ | ○ | ✳✳✳
H 45cm (18in) S 30cm (1ft)
The foliage of this spiky-leaved, clump-forming plant is rather like that of an iris. The leaves are grey-green and edged with white or creamy yellow. The upright stems are clothed with many small, creamy-yellow flowers. Grow in moderately fertile, well-drained soil.

Soleirolia soleirolii
Perennial
🌿 | ◐● | ✳✳
H 4cm (1½in) S to 90cm (3ft)
Mind-your-own-business is a mat-forming plant with very tiny leaves that form a dense carpet of fresh green foliage. It is useful as a groundcover and in containers, but can be invasive and hard to get rid of. Grow in moisture-retentive soil.

Spiraea 'Arguta'
Shrub
🌿 | ❶ | ○◐ | ✳✳✳
H 1.8m (6ft) S 1.5m (5ft)
Forming an upright dome-shape, the arching branches of bridal wreath are smothered with heads of pure white flowers, making a spectacular display. Grow in moderately fertile, moist but well-drained soil.

Stachys byzantina 'Silver Carpet'
Perennial
🌿 | ○ | ✳✳✳
H 45cm (18in) S 60cm (2ft)
The only non-flowering variety of this species, it forms a ground-covering carpet of the woolly-textured, silver leaves that give it its name of lamb's ears. Grow in very well-drained soil.

Taxus baccata
Conifer
🌿 | ○● | ✳✳✳
H and S 2.4m (8ft)
An excellent specimen or hedging plant with narrow, dark green leaves, yew is relatively slow growing but responds to trimming and shaping. Grow on any well-drained soil.

Teucrium fruticans
Shrub
🌿 | ❷ | ○ | ✳✳
H 1.5m (5ft) S 1.2m (4ft)
The arching stems of shrubby germander are clothed with slender grey-green leaves that make an attractive background to its pale blue flowers. Can be trained closely against a wall or fence. Grow in well-drained soil, preferably neutral to alkaline.

Thuja occidentalis 'Rheingold'
Conifer
🌿 | ○ | ✳✳✳
H 1.2m (4ft) S 90cm (3ft)
Broadly conical in shape, this bush has golden-yellow leaves that turn rich old gold in winter. Grow in moist but well drained soil.

Tradescantia 'Purple Sabre'
Perennial
🌿 | ❷ | ◐ | ✳
H 15cm (6in) S 45cm (18in)
A spreading, trailing plant with large, broad, purple leaves that bears clusters of small pink flowers. Grow in fertile, moist but well-drained soil.

Tropaeolum speciosum
Climber
🌿 | ❷ | ○◐ | ✳✳✳
H to 3m (10ft)
Flame creeper is a slender-stemmed scrambler that bears masses of dark red, long-spurred flowers and has divided fresh green leaves. It prefers sun but likes its roots in shade. Grow in moist, humus-rich, acid soil.

Tulipa
Bulb
🌿 | ❶ | ○ | ✳✳✳
H variable S variable
Orange varieties include 'Generaal de Wet', 'Orange Favourite' and 'Orange Monarch'. Striking, dark purple or maroon-purple flowers are found on the double-flowered 'Black Hero' and 'Queen of the Night'. *T. praestans* 'Fusilier' and *T.* 'Red Riding Hood' are red. Yellow-flowered varieties include 'Georgette', 'Golden Apeldoorn', 'Golden Emperor' and 'Texas Gold'. Grow in fertile, well-drained soil and in a sheltered site.

Verbena bonariensis
Perennial
🌿 | ❷-❸ | ○ | ✳✳
H 1.5m (5ft) S 45cm (18in)
This plant's graceful, open-branched, tall stems are topped with flat heads of violet-purple flowers, which attract bees. Grow in moderately fertile, moist but well-drained soil.

Veronica peduncularis 'Georgia Blue'
Perennial
🌿 | ❶-❷ | ○◐ | ✳✳✳
H 15cm (6in) S 60cm (2ft)
This vigorous, long-flowering veronica forms a spreading carpet of small leaves and produces many racemes of small, very deep blue flowers. Grow on light, moderately fertile soil.

Viburnum
Shrub
🌿 or 🌿 | ❶-❷ | ○◐ | ✳✳✳
H and S 1.2m (4ft)
The rounded *Viburnum* x *juddii* bears very large, round heads of white, strongly scented flowers in late spring and early summer. Grow in moderately fertile, moist but well-drained soil. *Viburnum davidii* forms a neat, wide-spreading mound of large, dark green, leathery leaves that have an attractive ridged surface and are evergreen. Tiny white flowers are borne in clusters. Grow on moist but well-drained soil.

Vinca minor
Shrub
🌿 | ❶ | ○● | ✳✳✳
H 15cm (6in) S to 90cm (3ft)
Lesser periwinkles are tough and useful as groundcover. They bear many open, clear blue flowers against dark green foliage, and forming a spreading carpet of stems that root as they go. Grow them in any reasonably fertile, well-drained soil. *V.m.* 'Variegata' has pointed green leaves, which are widely edged with creamy white and produces large, deep blue flowers along the stems. *V.m.* 'Illumination' is the most showy of the periwinkles, with green, oval leaves that have a very bright gold centre and deep blue flowers. Grow in all but very dry soil.

Viola riviniana 'Purpurea Group'
Perennial
🌿 | ❶-❷ | ○● | ✳✳✳
H 10cm (4in) S 15cm (6in)
The purple-leaved violet forms small, spreading clumps of rounded to heart-shaped purple leaves, and bears small, light purple flowers on short stems. It self-seeds readily and grows in most soils but prefers one that is humus-rich and moist but well drained.

index

Page numbers in *italic* refer to the illustrations

acknowledgements

Photographic acknowledgements in source order

Mark Bolton 31 centre, 31 Bottom, 37, 47 bottom left, 57, 71 Top, 71 bottom left/Hadspen Garden 15 Top/Lady Farm, Somerset 18/Maurice Green, Leamington Spa, UK 76

Garden Picture Library/Chris Burrows 31 top right/David Cavagnaro 82/Ron Evans 43 top left/John Glover 23 centre left, 39 bottom/Neil Holmes 27 centre left, 40 right, 43 top right/Jerry Pavia 47 centre left/Howard Rice 31 centre right, 39 centre right, 83 Top, 98 Top/JS Sira 60 centre/Georgia Glynn-Smith 67 right/Janet Sorrell 47 bottom right/Sunniva Harte 27 centre right/Juliette Wade 27 top left/Didier Willery 27 Bottom/Steve Wooster 97 top

Octopus Publishing Group Limited 30, 31 centre left, 48 left, 48 right, 62, 96/Mark Bolton 2, 5 top, 5 bottom, 9, 10, 13 top right, 13 bottom left, 15 bottom left, 22, 53 top, 77 top, 78, 84, 109 bottom, 110, 111 top, 111 bottom, 114, 115 bottom right, 121 bottom/Michael Boys 32 left, 41, 42, 95 Bottom Right/Jerry Harpur 15 bottom right, 23 top right, 32 right, 33, 39 centre left, 50, 55 bottom, 61, 66, 93 bottom, 98 bottom/Marcus Harpur 14 Wol and Sue Staines, Glen Chantry, Essex, 16, 17 top left, 17 centre right, 17 bottom, 19 right, 20, 23 bottom left RHS Wisley, 24, 26, 28 top, 28 bottom, 34, 36 bottom, 36 top, 38, 44 top, 45, 46, 53 bottom, 55 top left, 55 top right, 74, 77 bottom, 79, 80, 83 bottom, 87 top, 87 bottom, 88, 90 top, 90 bottom, 91 left, 91 right, 92, 93 top, 94, 100, 101 left, 102, 103 left, 103 right, 108, 116, 118, 119 right, 120, 128-129, 130/Andrew Lawson 23 top left, 24 left, 27 centre, 27 top right, 29, 35 centre left, 35 bottom left, 39 top left/Peter Myers 81 bottom/Howard Rice 64 left, 64 right/David Sarton 4, 7, 8 left, 8 right, 52, 56 right, 81 top, 85 bottom, 104, 113 bottom, 119 left, 121 top, 122-123/Mark Winwood 97 bottom/Steve Wooster 56 left/George Wright 23 Centre Right, 24 right, 25, 40 left, 44 bottom, 49, 63 left, 68, 101 right

Jerry Harpur 43 centre left, 43 Bottom, 72 right/Beth Chatto 126-127/Bob Dash 109 right/Chaumont 112, 113 centre/Dan Pearson, London 113 top/Des; Arabella Lennox-Boyd/RHS Chelsea 70/Longwood, Philadelphia 124-125/Rob Sterk, Amsterdam, Holland 115 top

Marcus Harpur 59 left, 95 bottom left

Andrew Lawson 35 centre right, 35 bottom right, 39 top right, 43 centre, 43 centre right, 54, 58, 60 right, 63 right, 69, 71 bottom right, 72 left, 73/Des; Arabella Lennox-Boyd 19 top left/Des; Simon Shire 115 bottom left/Lawhead Croft 86/Sticky Wicket, Dorset 12

S & O Mathews 35 top, 39 centre, 47 centre right, 60 left /Meon Orchard, Hampshire 99 /RHS Wisley 59 right

Clive Nichols 23 bottom centre left, 31 top left, 35 centre, 47 top/Carol Klein, Chelsea 99 65/Christopher Bradley-Hole 107 top left/Lisette Pleasance 85 top/Roger Platts 67 left/Robin Green, Ralph Cade, London 106/The Nichol's Garden, Reading 107 bottom, 109 top left

Supplied by Noack Roses 47 centre

Executive Editor Sarah Ford
Editorial Manager Jane Birch
Executive Art Editor Peter Burt
Designer Geoff Borin
Production Controller Louise Hall
Picture Research Christine Junemann